The Curse of Dracula™

THE CURSE OF DRACULA™

Story by · MARV WOLFMAN

Art by · GENE COLAN

Colors by · DAVE STEWART

Letters by · RICHARD STARKINGS
& COMICRAFT

DARK HORSE BOOKS™

Publisher
MIKE RICHARDSON

Editor
SCOTT ALLIE

Assistant Editors
MATT DRYER AND DAVE MARSHALL

Collection Designer
TINA ALESSI

Art Director
LIA RIBACCHI

PUBLISHED BY
DARK HORSE BOOKS
A DIVISION OF
DARK HORSE COMICS, INC.
10956 SE MAIN STREET
MILWAUKIE, OR 97222

DARKHORSE.COM

TO FIND A COMICS SHOP IN YOUR AREA, CALL THE COMIC
SHOP LOCATOR SERVICE TOLL-FREE AT 1-888-266-4226

FIRST EDITION: OCTOBER 2005
ISBN: 1-59307-391-7

10 9 8 7 6 5 4 3 2 1
PRINTED IN CHINA

THE CURSE OF DRACULA

THIS VOLUME COLLECTS ISSUES ONE THROUGH THREE OF
THE DARK HORSE COMIC-BOOK SERIES *THE CURSE OF DRACULA*.

Curses!

By Marv Wolfman

There is something about writing horror that forces me to do my best work. When you write horror or even comedy, you're not just fitting puzzle parts together, you're forced to go for something more. To succeed with horror you have to scare people. To succeed with comedy, you need to make them laugh. Fail to do either and the story fails.

Mystery stories are mainly intellectual exercises: Fit murderer A into crime scene B and mix in detective C and see how long it takes before C figures out who A is. No matter what the story is actually about, or how many troubles the hero has to go through or personal changes he/she makes during the adventure, it ultimately comes down to that quasi-mathematical formula. Superhero tales are the same: Villain A is out to get/destroy item B and superhero C has to stop him. Whether he does or he doesn't, the stories are essentially: what does it take to stop the bad guy?

We've seen that formula in so many variations of both that the writer knows he is probably not going to fool the reader. Instead, the writer puts together the plot pieces like a jigsaw puzzle, inserting action here or a plot twist there and hopes it moves fast enough and the characters are interesting enough to keep the readers turning the page. These stories, no matter how emotional they may be, still mainly appeal to the mind: Solve the problem. Complete the puzzle.

With a superhero story the reader instinctively knows it's not real, but they enjoy how the writer puts together plot, action, and character. With a mystery story the reader is trying to second-guess where the writer is leading them. Even a poor story is too often acceptable if it has enough action or thrills.

But in horror the writer has to draw the reader in, to connect not only with their fears but all people's common dreads. There is no simple mathematical formula unless it's frighten reader A with whatever B is. But horror appeals to the gut. It makes you suspend your intellect and go with your most primal instincts. For that reason alone, where detective and superhero stories can be reduced to a formula—no matter how well done they are—horror can't be. Horror reaches for real emotion. It's not about problem solving but about ignoring reality. Horror demands you create a nightmare from which the reader cannot awaken. You can't just let someone read a horror story. They have to feel it.

I love writing horror stories, and I think it's evident that Gene Colan, my collaborator on the story you're either about to read or reread depending on whether you bought the original *Curse of Dracula* comics back in 1998, does too. Look at the pages in this collected edition and you will see his wonderfully shadowed faces draw you into their most tumultuous emotions.

The Curse of Dracula is a particular favorite of mine. For eight years I wrote a comic for Marvel called *The Tomb of Dracula*. Gene Colan, who was drawing the book for a year before I got there, was my collaborator there, too. Gene was already a master artist and longtime professional, whereas I was just beginning my comics career. If you haven't seen those books, Marvel Comics has recently reprinted all our stories in four low-priced, black-and-white editions.

For those eight years Gene and I experimented with all kinds of storytelling. We pushed the boundaries of what could be done in comics. Every month we fought tooth and nail with the Comics Code, the organization that controlled what could and could not be done in the comics of the time, to show that comics could and should be aimed at grownups and not just kids.

TOD received a number of awards. More importantly, we connected with the growing comics audience of the time. Gene and I go to many conventions, and we still hear how important those early books were to so many of the readers. That the Marvel reprints have been selling like those proverbial hotcakes thirty years after we wrote them says something about how we connected with our readership.

Many characters came out of *TOD* that went on to their own fame. Blade the Vampire Hunter, a character I had come up with a year or so before I came to Marvel, was turned into a hit movie starring Wesley Snipes. It also featured a second character we created, Deacon Frost, the vampire who turned Blade into what he became. Two more Blade movies followed and both did extremely well at the box office. The third movie featured a version of Hannibal King, another of our creations.

But all good things come to an end, and *Tomb of Dracula* faded for the most part from our lives back in 1980.

Time passed. Continents sank. Mountains rose. Well, maybe not that much time passed, but I went on to co-create titles such as *New Teen Titans*, *Deathstroke the Terminator*, and *Crisis on Infinite Earths*, along with a horror title called *Night Force*, illustrated by, yes, Gene Colan, my favorite horror-collaborator. Beside *Night Force*, Gene went on to draw comics such as *Batman*, *Superman*, and many others.

In the mid to late 1990s, Mike Richardson, the publisher of Dark Horse Comics, and an old *Tomb of Dracula* fan, sought me out at the San Diego Comic Convention and asked if I'd like to work with Gene on a brand-new Dracula mini-series, one we would own this time.

I said yes, and immediately went to work to create not a doppelganger of the *Tomb of Dracula* cast, but all-new characters set in a very different and much more realistic and troubled world. Dracula's pursuers are not powerful heroes carved out of the classic good-guy mold; these people have suffered greatly because of their cause and the terrible lives they've been forced to lead, and those pains come out in everything they do and say.

Our leader, Jonathan Van Helsing, grandson of Abraham from Bram Stoker's original *Dracula* novel, is a quiet, dour man who prays before every battle. He raises the money to continue his obsessive battle by writing books and lecturing on the monsters who walk among us.

The blind half-Japanese woman Hiro was raped and had her eyes gouged out by vampires after being tortured for more than a month. Today there is so much vampire blood in her she "sees" like a bat and can sense vampires from a great distance.

The Spaniard Simon (no last name given) watched the criminal gang he worked for be destroyed by vampires. He barely managed to escape with his life. He knows the vampires want to finish the job and kill him, but he intends to destroy them first.

Nikita Kazan, the former Russian KGB agent, worked security for the top-secret Russian parapsychology experiments of the '80s and '90s. After a vampire den invaded the facility and killed his family, Kazan joined Van Helsing and the others to seek revenge.

Dracula himself is portrayed as a dark evil, but one who, like the snake in Eden, hides behind a sinister smile. The stories take place in today's world, and this new Dracula is concerned less with the constant hunt for blood (he has his mindless acolytes hunt for him) than with political power.

The violence in *Curse of Dracula* is not big movie-action fight scenes, but darker and much more insidious than anything we have done before. This is a world of shadows and evil, and even the battles have to reflect that grim reality.

There are lots of surprises in this story, even more than will be apparent when you read these stories in their first collected English edition. I'm hoping there will be enough of you picking up this book to warrant a second *Curse of Dracula* series. Gene and I began our story here, but there is still a lot more to tell.

—Marv Wolfman
April 6, 2005

Marv Wolfman's website can be found at www.marvwolfman.com. Gene Colan's website can be found at www.genecolan.com.

Chapter I

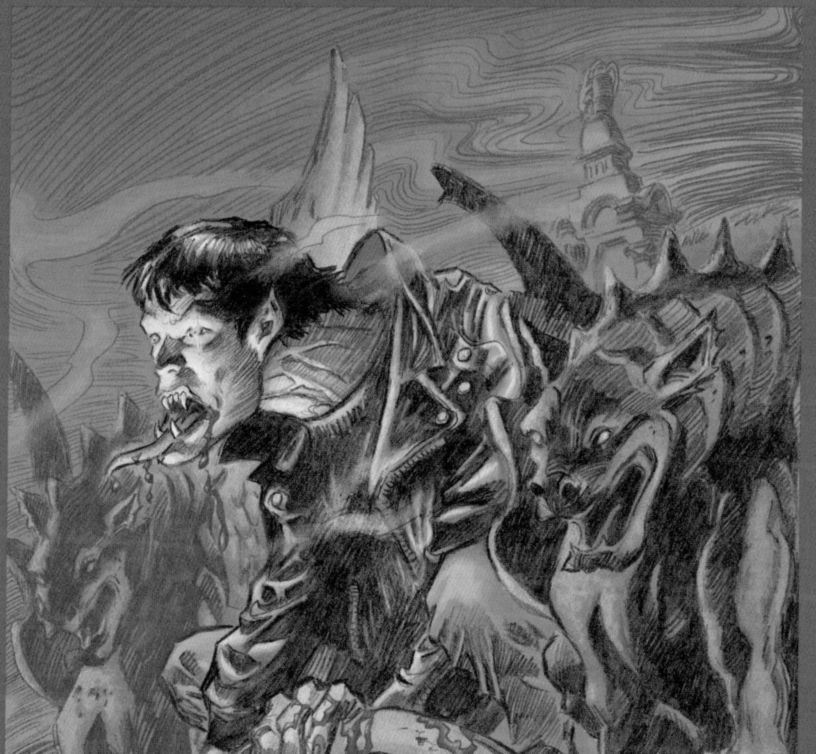
1110
Gene Colan

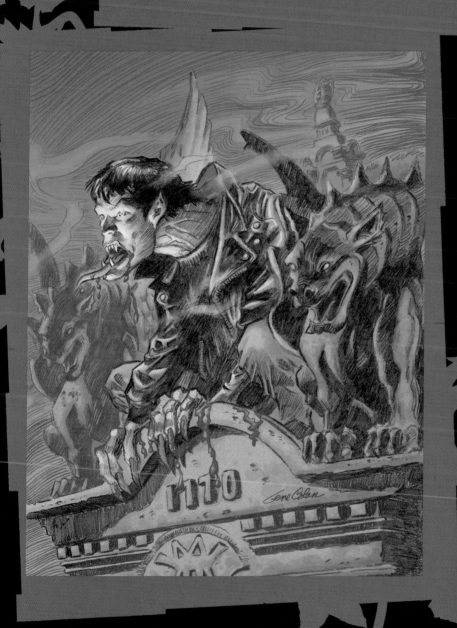

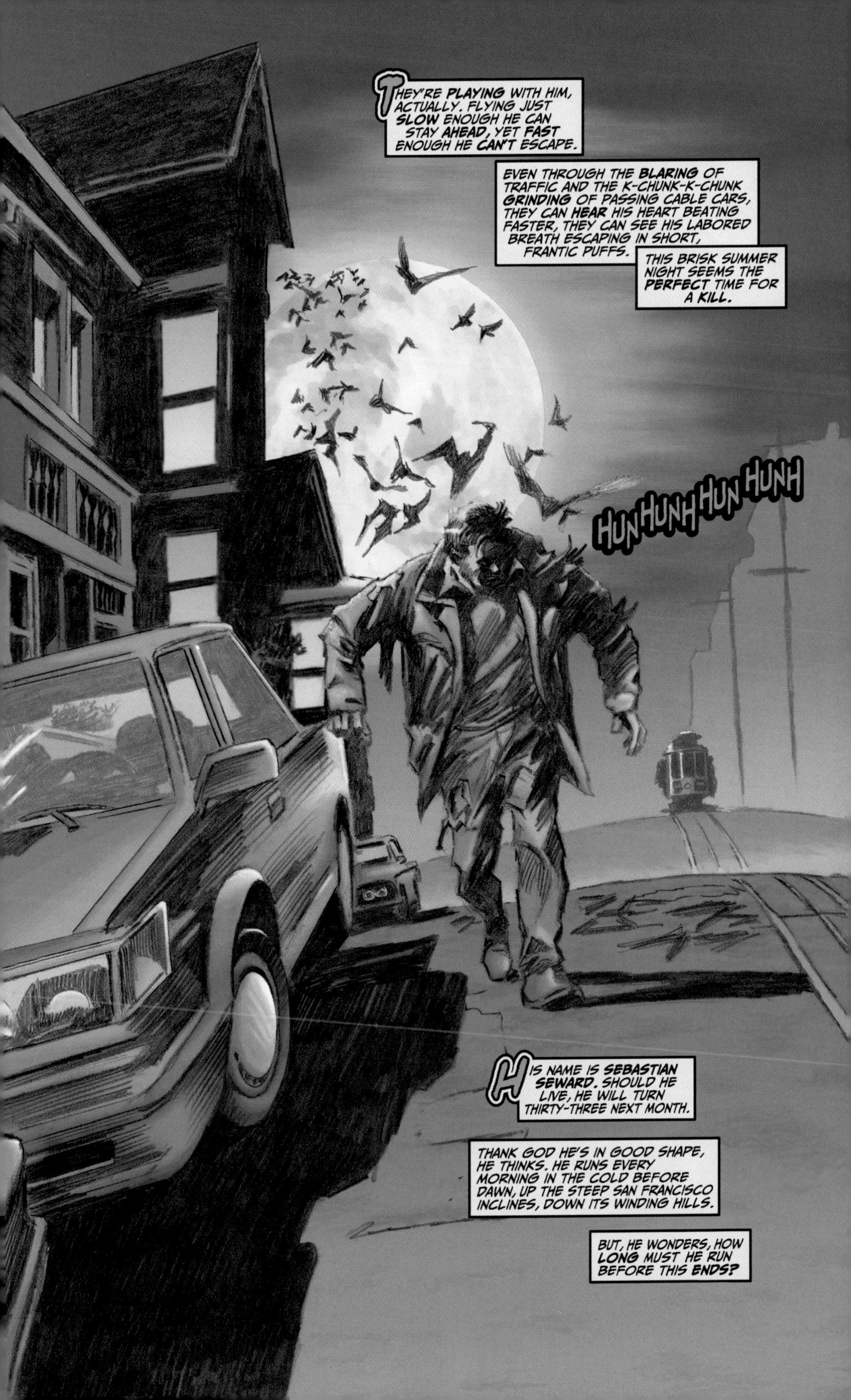
THEY'RE PLAYING WITH HIM, ACTUALLY. FLYING JUST SLOW ENOUGH HE CAN STAY AHEAD, YET FAST ENOUGH HE CAN'T ESCAPE.
EVEN THROUGH THE BLARING OF TRAFFIC AND THE K-CHUNK-K-CHUNK GRINDING OF PASSING CABLE CARS, THEY CAN HEAR HIS HEART BEATING FASTER, THEY CAN SEE HIS LABORED BREATH ESCAPING IN SHORT, FRANTIC PUFFS.
THIS BRISK SUMMER NIGHT SEEMS THE PERFECT TIME FOR A KILL.
HUN HUNH HUN HUNH
HIS NAME IS SEBASTIAN SEWARD. SHOULD HE LIVE, HE WILL TURN THIRTY-THREE NEXT MONTH.
THANK GOD HE'S IN GOOD SHAPE, HE THINKS. HE RUNS EVERY MORNING IN THE COLD BEFORE DAWN, UP THE STEEP SAN FRANCISCO INCLINES, DOWN ITS WINDING HILLS.
BUT, HE WONDERS, HOW LONG MUST HE RUN BEFORE THIS ENDS?

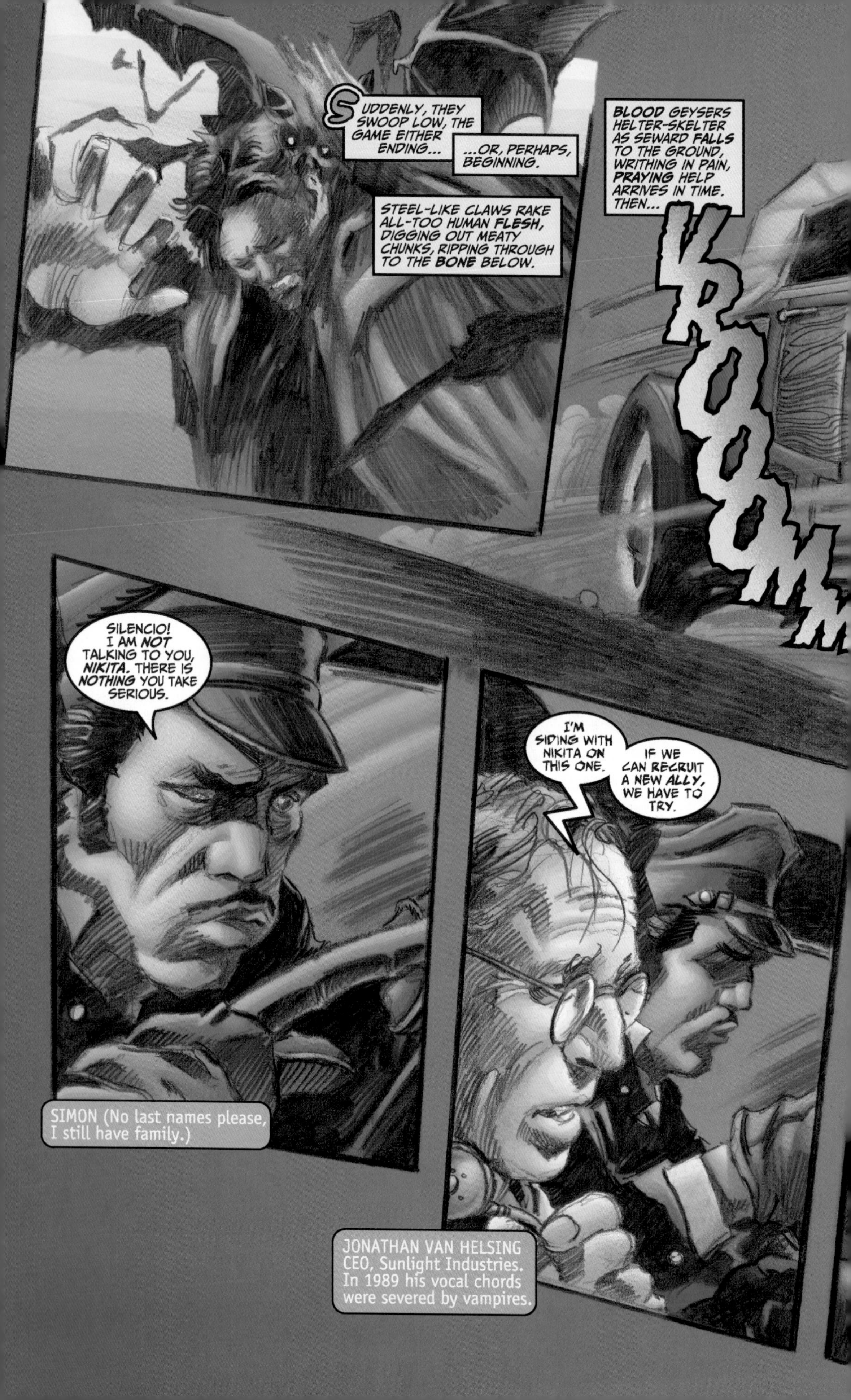
SUDDENLY, THEY SWOOP LOW, THE GAME EITHER ENDING...
...OR, PERHAPS, BEGINNING.
STEEL-LIKE CLAWS RAKE ALL-TOO HUMAN FLESH, DIGGING OUT MEATY CHUNKS, RIPPING THROUGH TO THE BONE BELOW.
BLOOD GEYSERS HELTER-SKELTER AS SEWARD FALLS TO THE GROUND, WRITHING IN PAIN, PRAYING HELP ARRIVES IN TIME. THEN...
VROOOM
SILENCIO! I AM NOT TALKING TO YOU, NIKITA. THERE IS NOTHING YOU TAKE SERIOUS.
SIMON (No last names please, I still have family.)
I'M SIDING WITH NIKITA ON THIS ONE.
IF WE CAN RECRUIT A NEW ALLY, WE HAVE TO TRY.
JONATHAN VAN HELSING CEO, Sunlight Industries. In 1989 his vocal chords were severed by vampires.

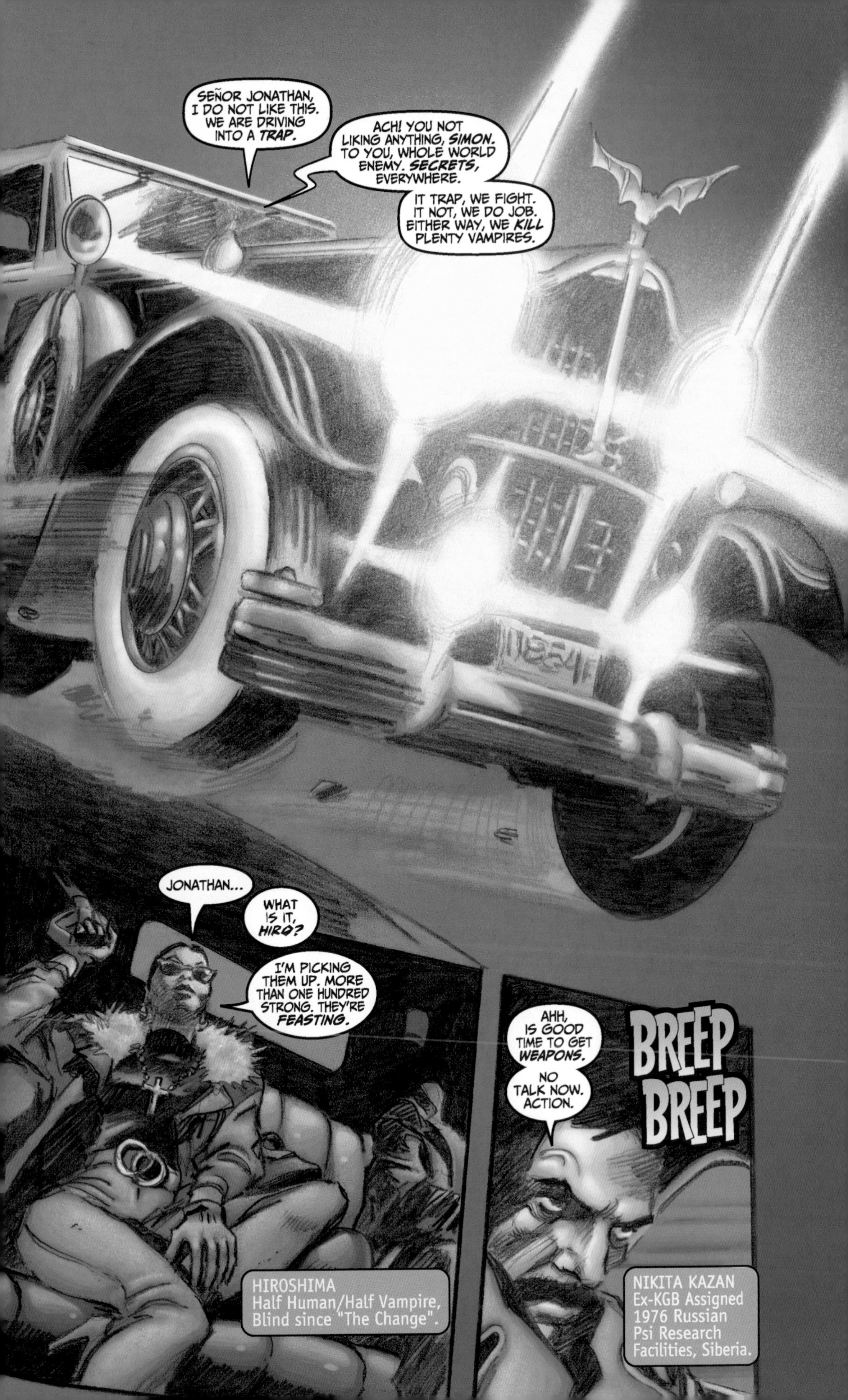
SEÑOR JONATHAN, I DO NOT LIKE THIS. WE ARE DRIVING INTO A TRAP.
ACH! YOU NOT LIKING ANYTHING, SIMON. TO YOU, WHOLE WORLD ENEMY. SECRETS, EVERYWHERE.
IT TRAP, WE FIGHT. IT NOT, WE DO JOB. EITHER WAY, WE KILL PLENTY VAMPIRES.
JONATHAN...
WHAT IS IT, HIRO?
I'M PICKING THEM UP. MORE THAN ONE HUNDRED STRONG. THEY'RE FEASTING.
HIROSHIMA
Half Human/Half Vampire,
Blind since "The Change".
BREEP BREEP
AHH, IS GOOD TIME TO GET WEAPONS.
NO TALK NOW. ACTION.
NIKITA KAZAN
Ex-KGB Assigned
1976 Russian
Psi Research
Facilities, Siberia.

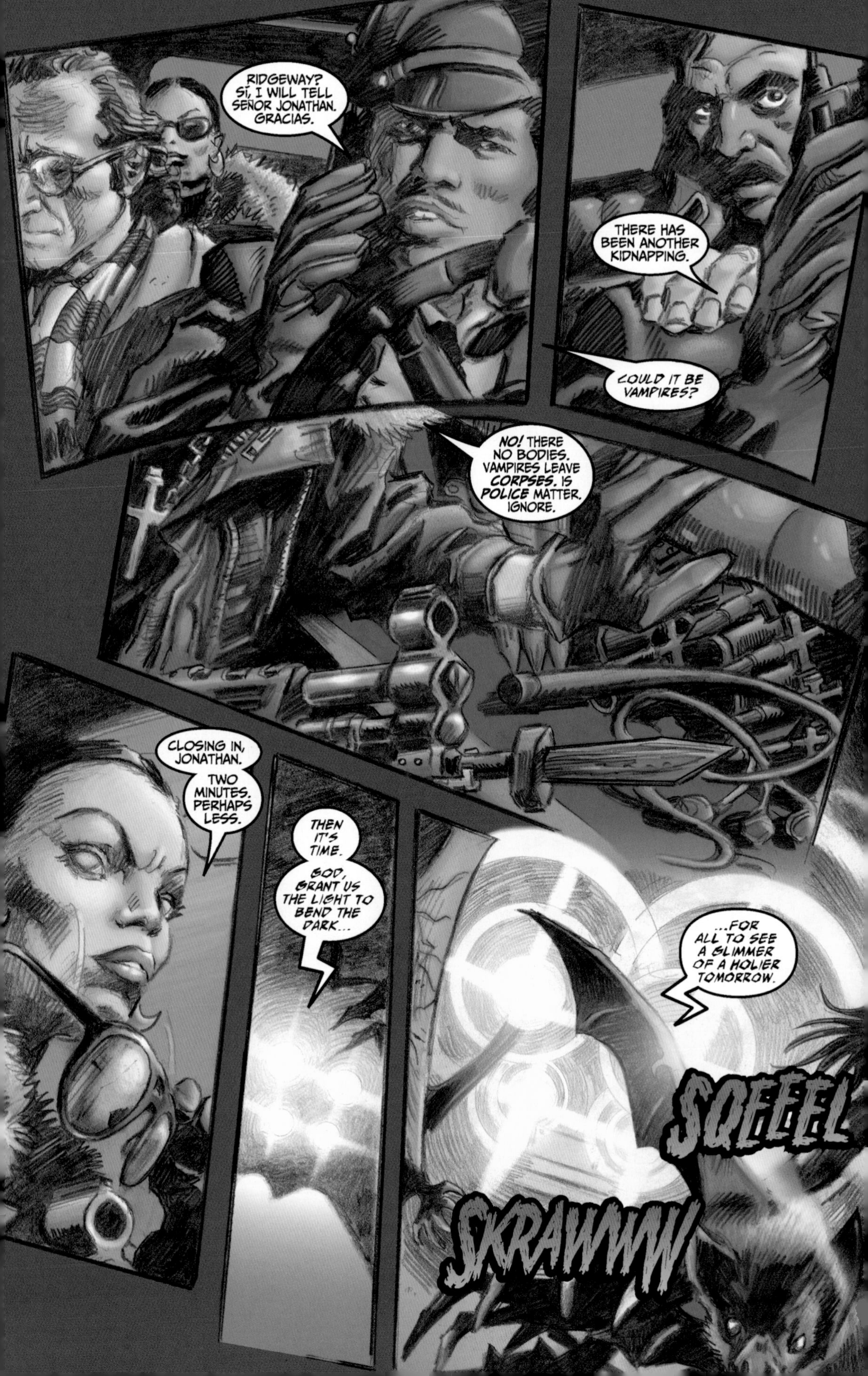
RIDGEWAY? SÍ, I WILL TELL SEÑOR JONATHAN. GRACIAS.
THERE HAS BEEN ANOTHER KIDNAPPING.
COULD IT BE VAMPIRES?
NO! THERE NO BODIES. VAMPIRES LEAVE CORPSES. IS POLICE MATTER. IGNORE.
CLOSING IN, JONATHAN.
TWO MINUTES. PERHAPS LESS.
THEN IT'S TIME.
GOD, GRANT US THE LIGHT TO BEND THE DARK...
...FOR ALL TO SEE A GLIMMER OF A HOLIER TOMORROW.
SQEEEL
SKRAWWW

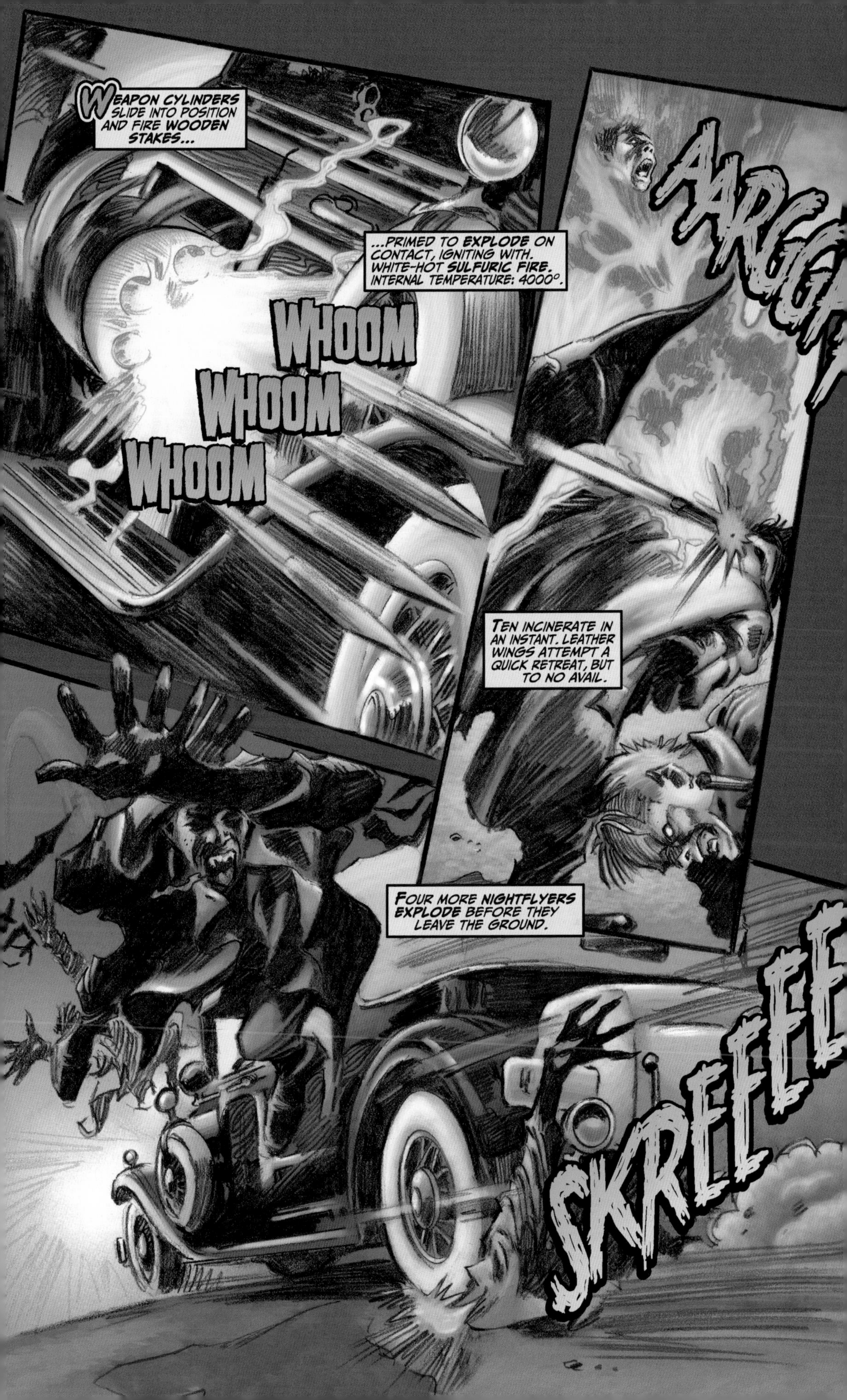
WEAPON CYLINDERS SLIDE INTO POSITION AND FIRE WOODEN STAKES...
...PRIMED TO EXPLODE ON CONTACT, IGNITING WITH. WHITE-HOT SULFURIC FIRE. INTERNAL TEMPERATURE: 4000°.
WHOOM
WHOOM
WHOOM
AARGG
TEN INCINERATE IN AN INSTANT. LEATHER WINGS ATTEMPT A QUICK RETREAT, BUT TO NO AVAIL.
FOUR MORE NIGHTFLYERS EXPLODE BEFORE THEY LEAVE THE GROUND.
SKREEEE

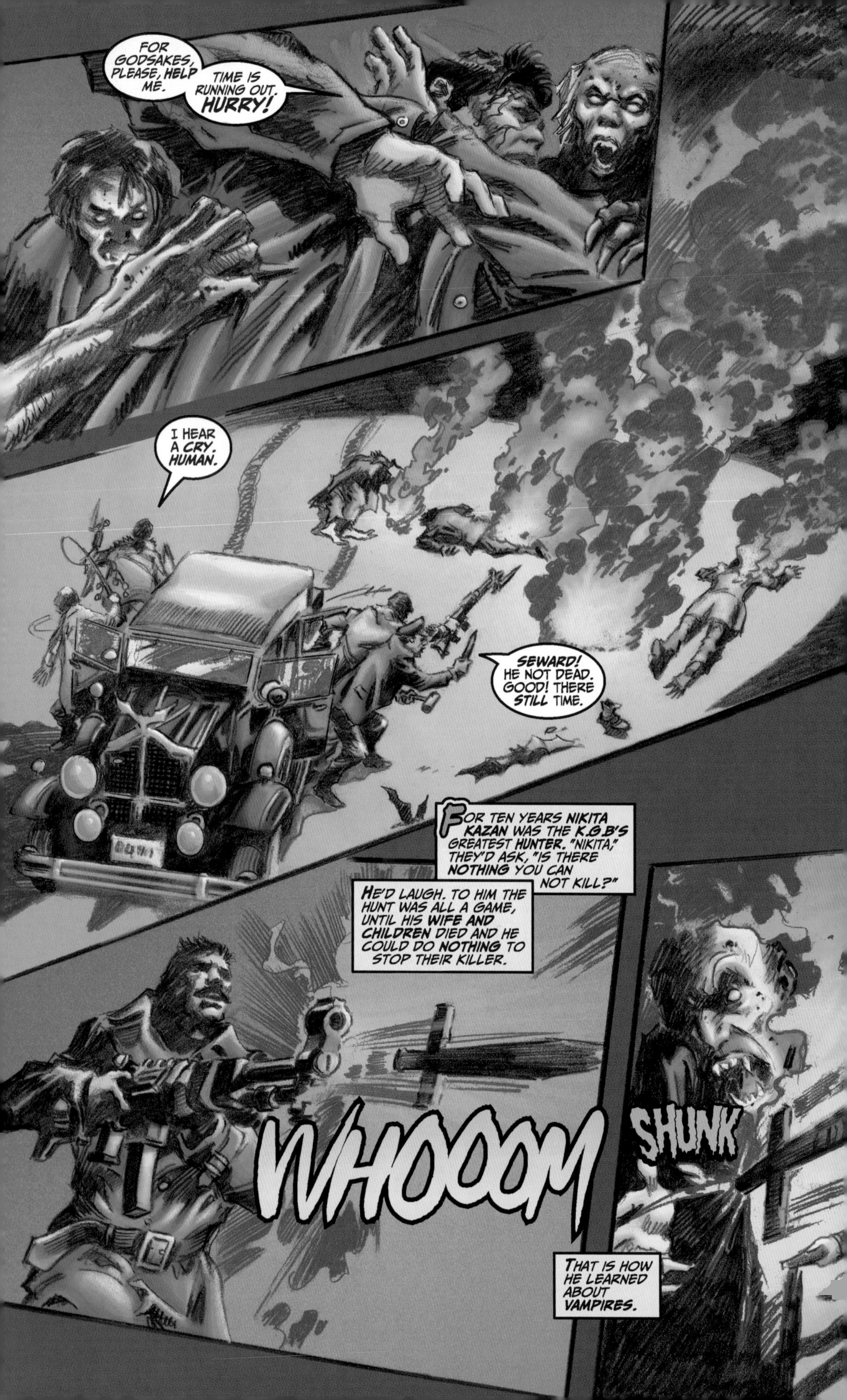
FOR GODSAKES, PLEASE, HELP ME.
TIME IS RUNNING OUT. HURRY!
I HEAR A CRY. HUMAN.
SEWARD! HE NOT DEAD. GOOD! THERE STILL TIME.
FOR TEN YEARS NIKITA KAZAN WAS THE K.G.B'S GREATEST HUNTER. "NIKITA," THEY'D ASK, "IS THERE NOTHING YOU CAN NOT KILL?"
HE'D LAUGH. TO HIM THE HUNT WAS ALL A GAME, UNTIL HIS WIFE AND CHILDREN DIED AND HE COULD DO NOTHING TO STOP THEIR KILLER.
WHOOOM
SHUNK
THAT IS HOW HE LEARNED ABOUT VAMPIRES.

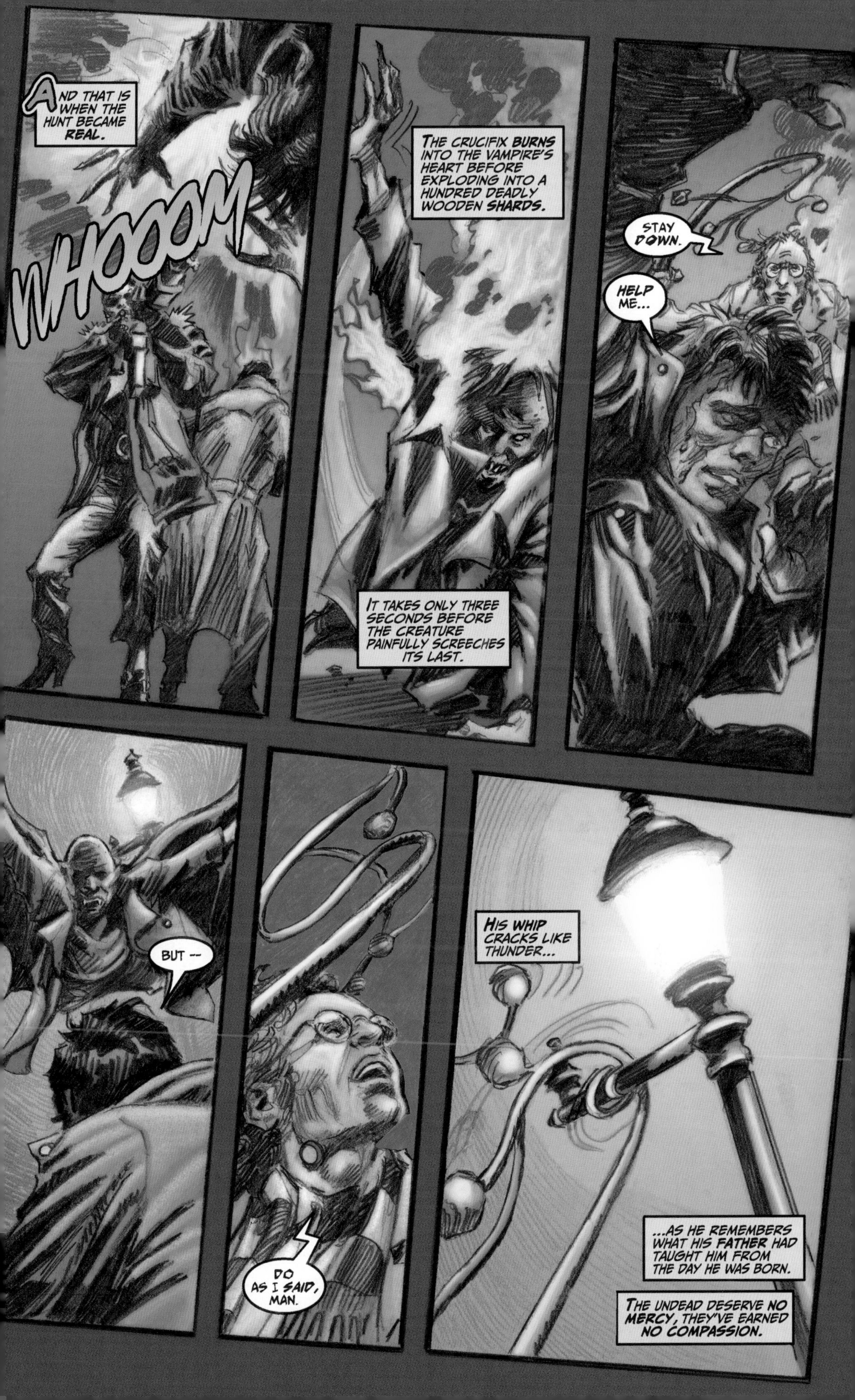

AND THAT IS WHEN THE HUNT BECAME REAL.
WHOOOM
THE CRUCIFIX BURNS INTO THE VAMPIRE'S HEART BEFORE EXPLODING INTO A HUNDRED DEADLY WOODEN SHARDS.
IT TAKES ONLY THREE SECONDS BEFORE THE CREATURE PAINFULLY SCREECHES ITS LAST.
STAY DOWN.
HELP ME...
BUT --
DO AS I SAID, MAN.
HIS WHIP CRACKS LIKE THUNDER...
...AS HE REMEMBERS WHAT HIS FATHER HAD TAUGHT HIM FROM THE DAY HE WAS BORN.
THE UNDEAD DESERVE NO MERCY, THEY'VE EARNED NO COMPASSION.

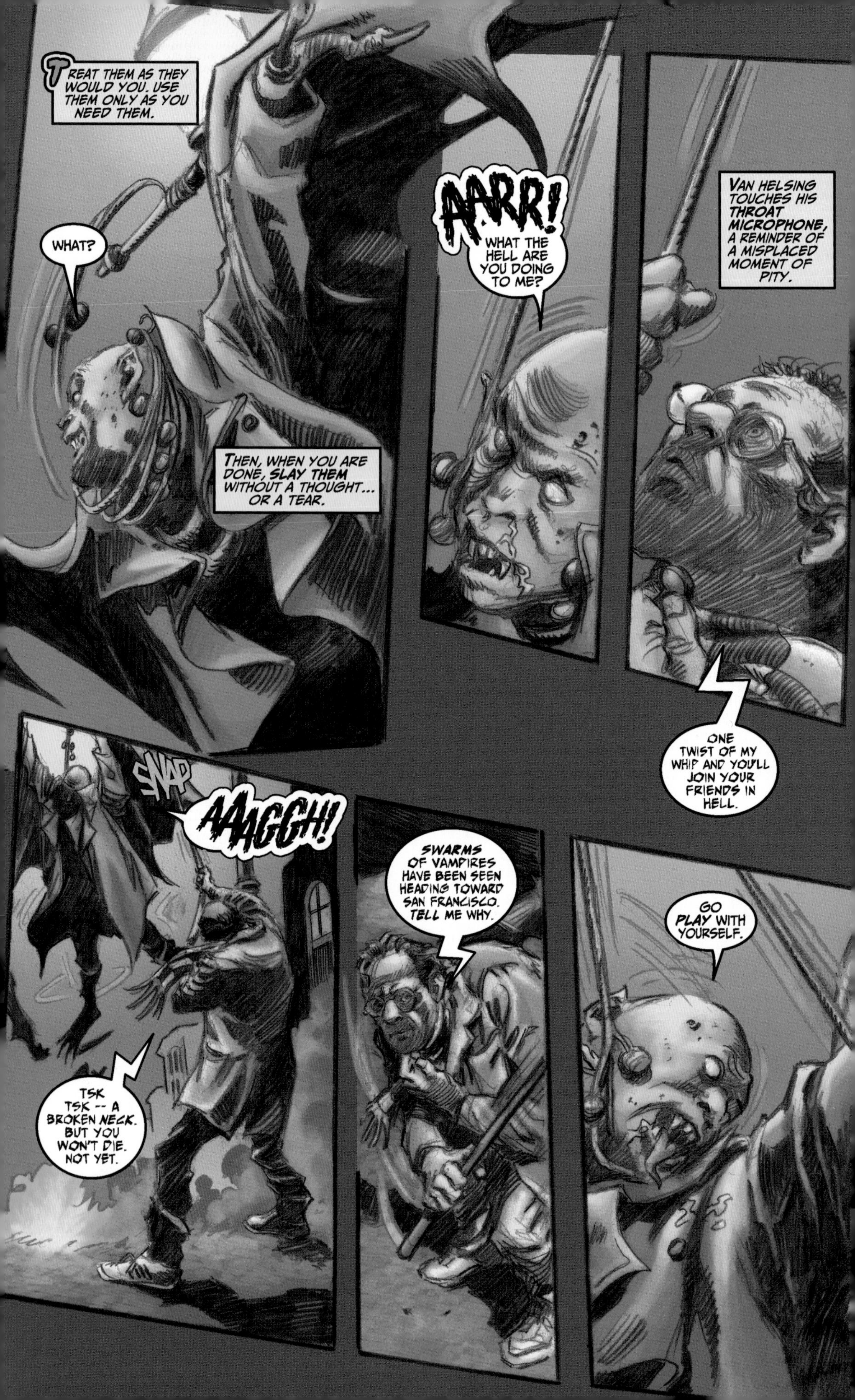
TREAT THEM AS THEY WOULD YOU. USE THEM ONLY AS YOU NEED THEM.
WHAT?
THEN, WHEN YOU ARE DONE, SLAY THEM WITHOUT A THOUGHT... OR A TEAR.
AARR!
WHAT THE HELL ARE YOU DOING TO ME?
VAN HELSING TOUCHES HIS THROAT MICROPHONE, A REMINDER OF A MISPLACED MOMENT OF PITY.
ONE TWIST OF MY WHIP AND YOU'LL JOIN YOUR FRIENDS IN HELL.
SNAP
AAAGGH!
TSK TSK -- A BROKEN NECK. BUT YOU WON'T DIE. NOT YET.
SWARMS OF VAMPIRES HAVE BEEN SEEN HEADING TOWARD SAN FRANCISCO. TELL ME WHY.
GO PLAY WITH YOURSELF.

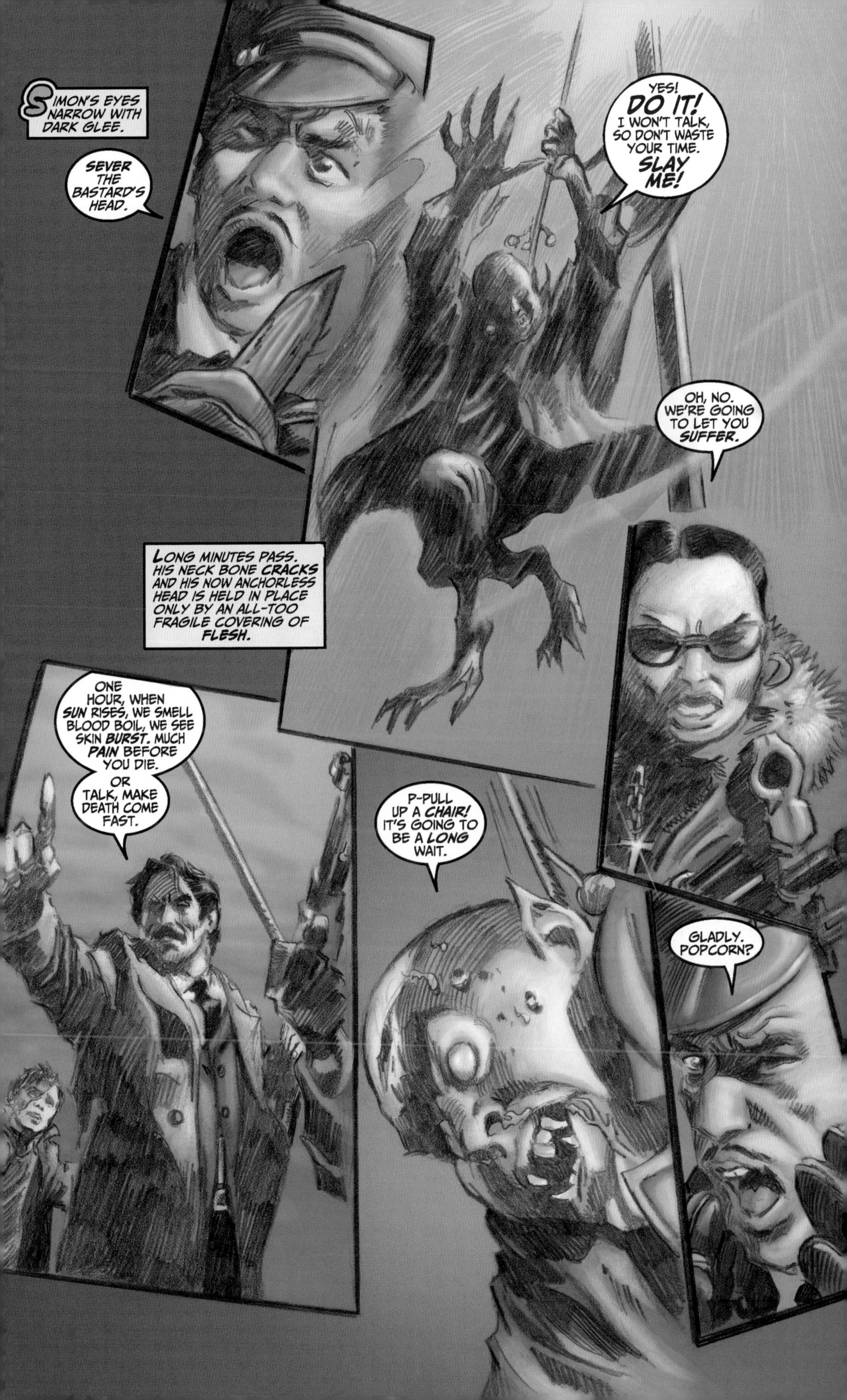
SIMON'S EYES NARROW WITH DARK GLEE.
SEVER THE BASTARD'S HEAD.
YES! DO IT! I WON'T TALK, SO DON'T WASTE YOUR TIME. SLAY ME!
OH, NO. WE'RE GOING TO LET YOU SUFFER.
LONG MINUTES PASS. HIS NECK BONE CRACKS AND HIS NOW ANCHORLESS HEAD IS HELD IN PLACE ONLY BY AN ALL-TOO FRAGILE COVERING OF FLESH.
ONE HOUR, WHEN SUN RISES, WE SMELL BLOOD BOIL, WE SEE SKIN BURST. MUCH PAIN BEFORE YOU DIE.
OR TALK, MAKE DEATH COME FAST.
P-PULL UP A CHAIR! IT'S GOING TO BE A LONG WAIT.
GLADLY. POPCORN?

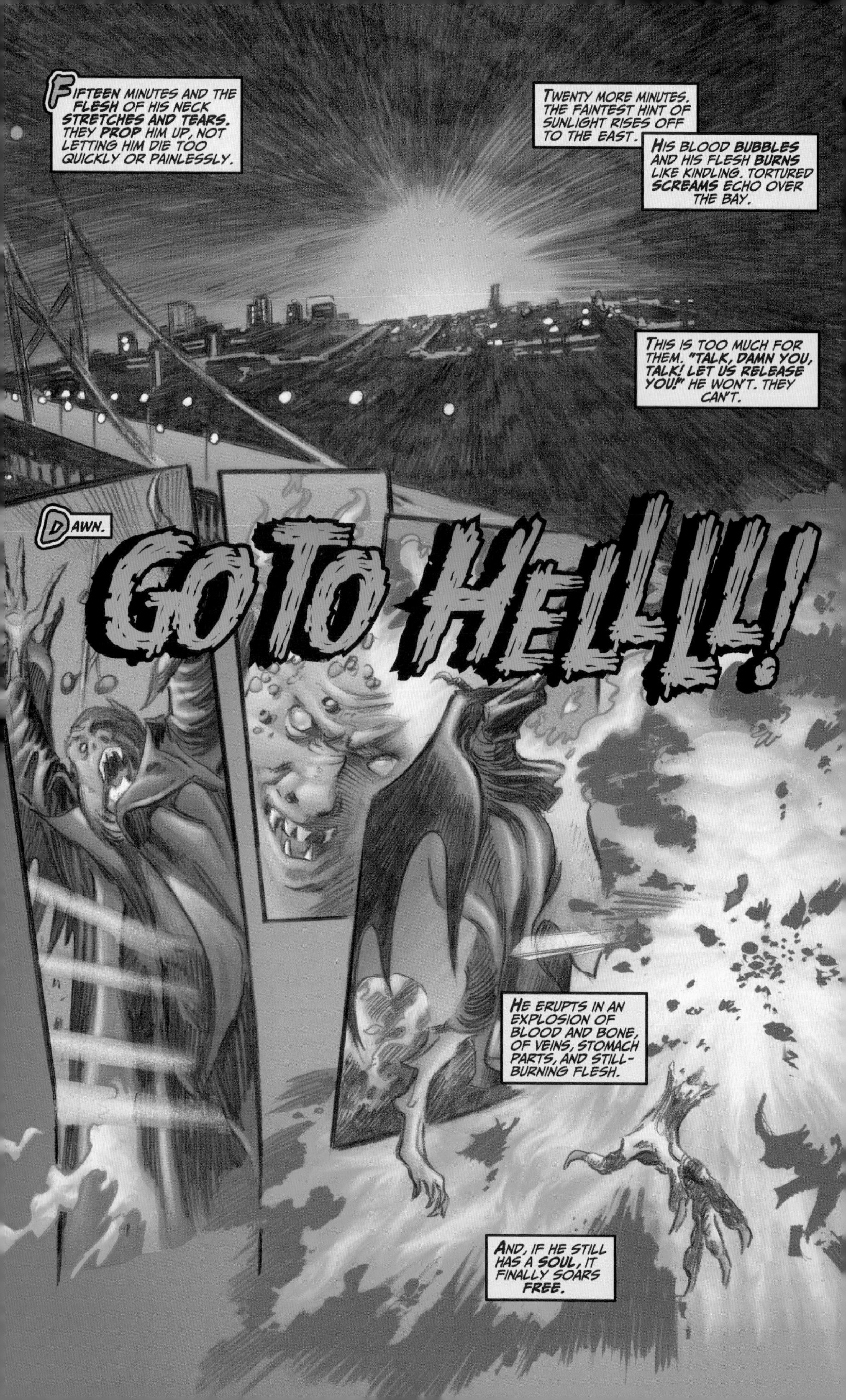
FIFTEEN MINUTES AND THE FLESH OF HIS NECK STRETCHES AND TEARS. THEY PROP HIM UP, NOT LETTING HIM DIE TOO QUICKLY OR PAINLESSLY.
TWENTY MORE MINUTES. THE FAINTEST HINT OF SUNLIGHT RISES OFF TO THE EAST.
HIS BLOOD BUBBLES AND HIS FLESH BURNS LIKE KINDLING. TORTURED SCREAMS ECHO OVER THE BAY.
THIS IS TOO MUCH FOR THEM. "TALK, DAMN YOU, TALK! LET US RELEASE YOU!" HE WON'T. THEY CAN'T.
DAWN.
GO TO HELL!!!
HE ERUPTS IN AN EXPLOSION OF BLOOD AND BONE, OF VEINS, STOMACH PARTS, AND STILL-BURNING FLESH.
AND, IF HE STILL HAS A SOUL, IT FINALLY SOARS FREE.

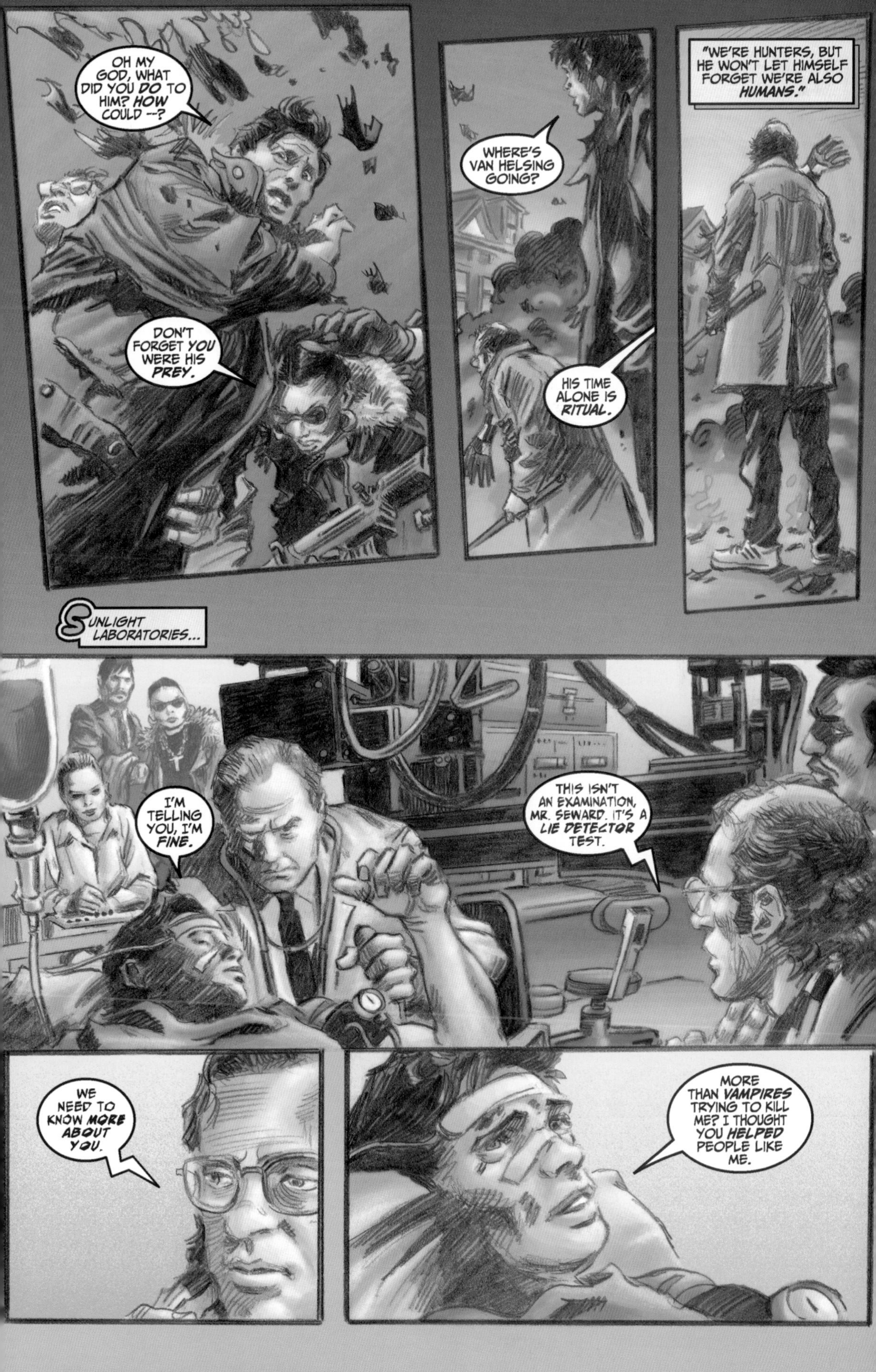
OH MY GOD, WHAT DID YOU DO TO HIM? HOW COULD --?
DON'T FORGET YOU WERE HIS PREY.
WHERE'S VAN HELSING GOING?
HIS TIME ALONE IS RITUAL.
"WE'RE HUNTERS, BUT HE WON'T LET HIMSELF FORGET WE'RE ALSO HUMANS."
SUNLIGHT LABORATORIES...
I'M TELLING YOU, I'M FINE.
THIS ISN'T AN EXAMINATION, MR. SEWARD. IT'S A LIE DETECTOR TEST.
WE NEED TO KNOW MORE ABOUT YOU.
MORE THAN VAMPIRES TRYING TO KILL ME? I THOUGHT YOU HELPED PEOPLE LIKE ME.

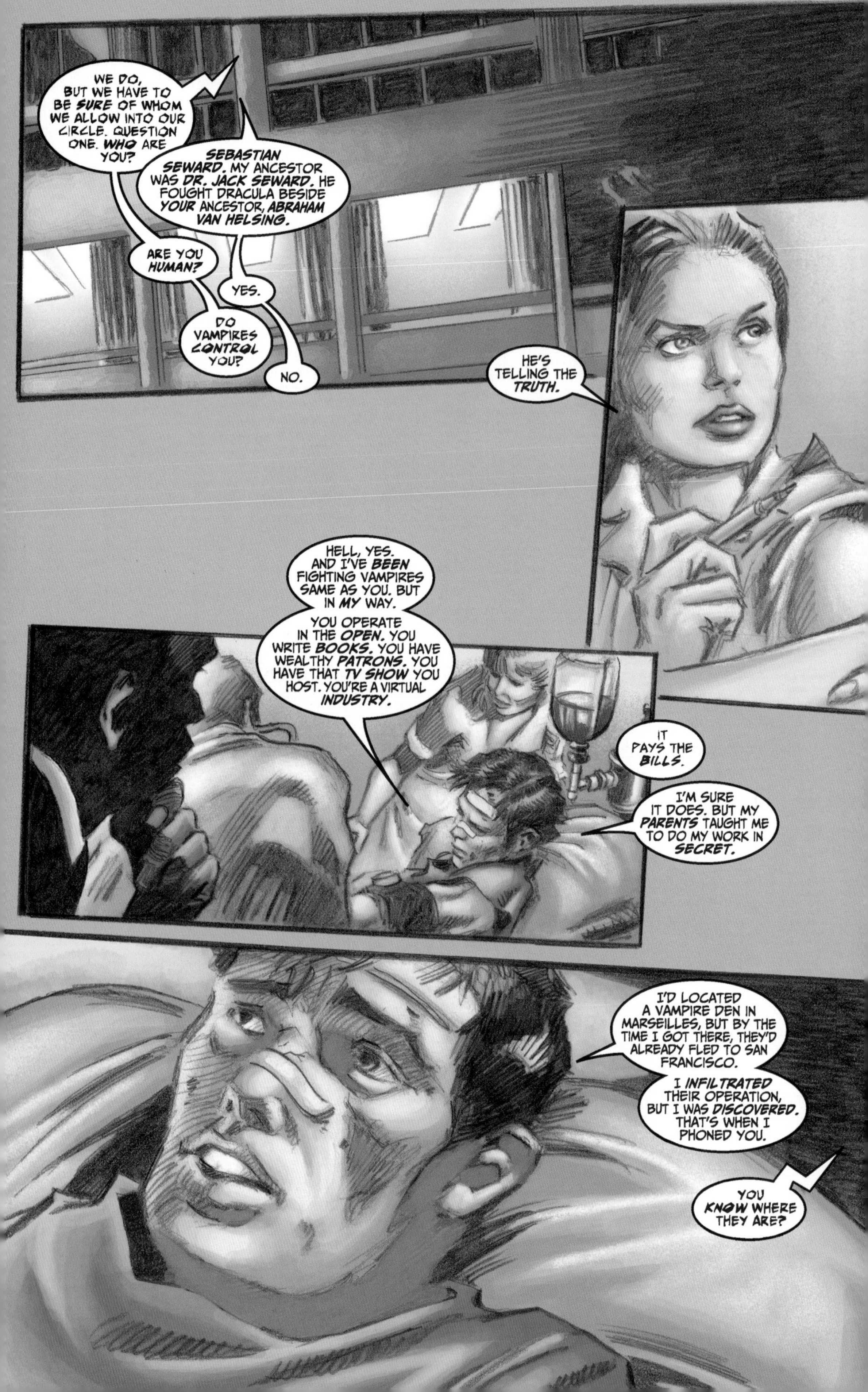
WE DO, BUT WE HAVE TO BE SURE OF WHOM WE ALLOW INTO OUR CIRCLE. QUESTION ONE. WHO ARE YOU?
SEBASTIAN SEWARD. MY ANCESTOR WAS DR. JACK SEWARD. HE FOUGHT DRACULA BESIDE YOUR ANCESTOR, ABRAHAM VAN HELSING.
ARE YOU HUMAN?
YES.
DO VAMPIRES CONTROL YOU?
NO.
HE'S TELLING THE TRUTH.
HELL, YES. AND I'VE BEEN FIGHTING VAMPIRES SAME AS YOU. BUT IN MY WAY.
YOU OPERATE IN THE OPEN. YOU WRITE BOOKS. YOU HAVE WEALTHY PATRONS. YOU HAVE THAT TV SHOW YOU HOST. YOU'RE A VIRTUAL INDUSTRY.
IT PAYS THE BILLS.
I'M SURE IT DOES. BUT MY PARENTS TAUGHT ME TO DO MY WORK IN SECRET.
I'D LOCATED A VAMPIRE DEN IN MARSEILLES, BUT BY THE TIME I GOT THERE, THEY'D ALREADY FLED TO SAN FRANCISCO.
I INFILTRATED THEIR OPERATION, BUT I WAS DISCOVERED. THAT'S WHEN I PHONED YOU.
YOU KNOW WHERE THEY ARE?

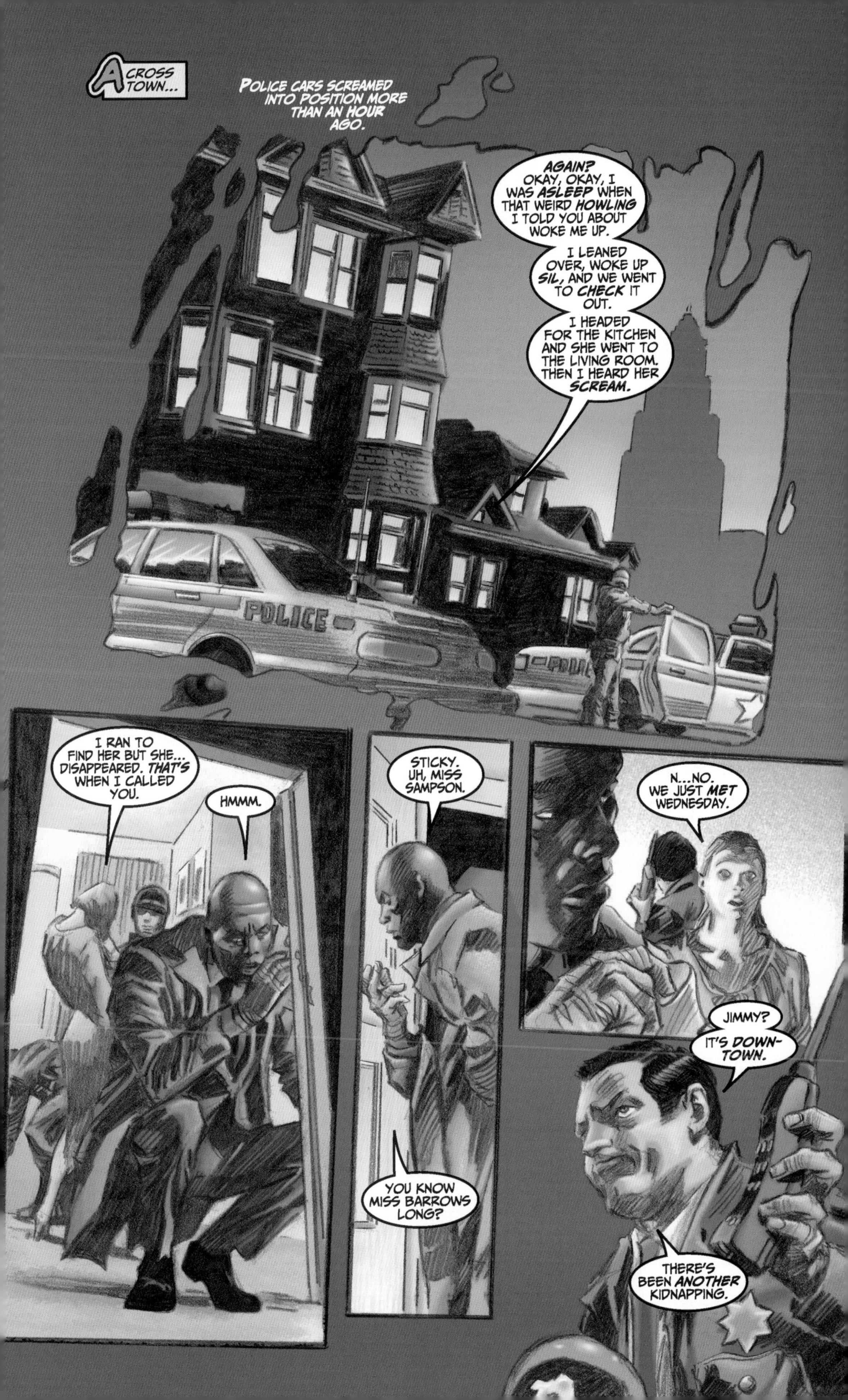
ACROSS TOWN...
POLICE CARS SCREAMED INTO POSITION MORE THAN AN HOUR AGO.
AGAIN? OKAY, OKAY, I WAS ASLEEP WHEN THAT WEIRD HOWLING I TOLD YOU ABOUT WOKE ME UP.
I LEANED OVER, WOKE UP SIL, AND WE WENT TO CHECK IT OUT.
I HEADED FOR THE KITCHEN AND SHE WENT TO THE LIVING ROOM. THEN I HEARD HER SCREAM.
POLICE
I RAN TO FIND HER BUT SHE... DISAPPEARED. THAT'S WHEN I CALLED YOU.
HMMM.
STICKY. UH, MISS SAMPSON.
YOU KNOW MISS BARROWS LONG?
N...NO. WE JUST MET WEDNESDAY.
JIMMY?
IT'S DOWNTOWN.
THERE'S BEEN ANOTHER KIDNAPPING.

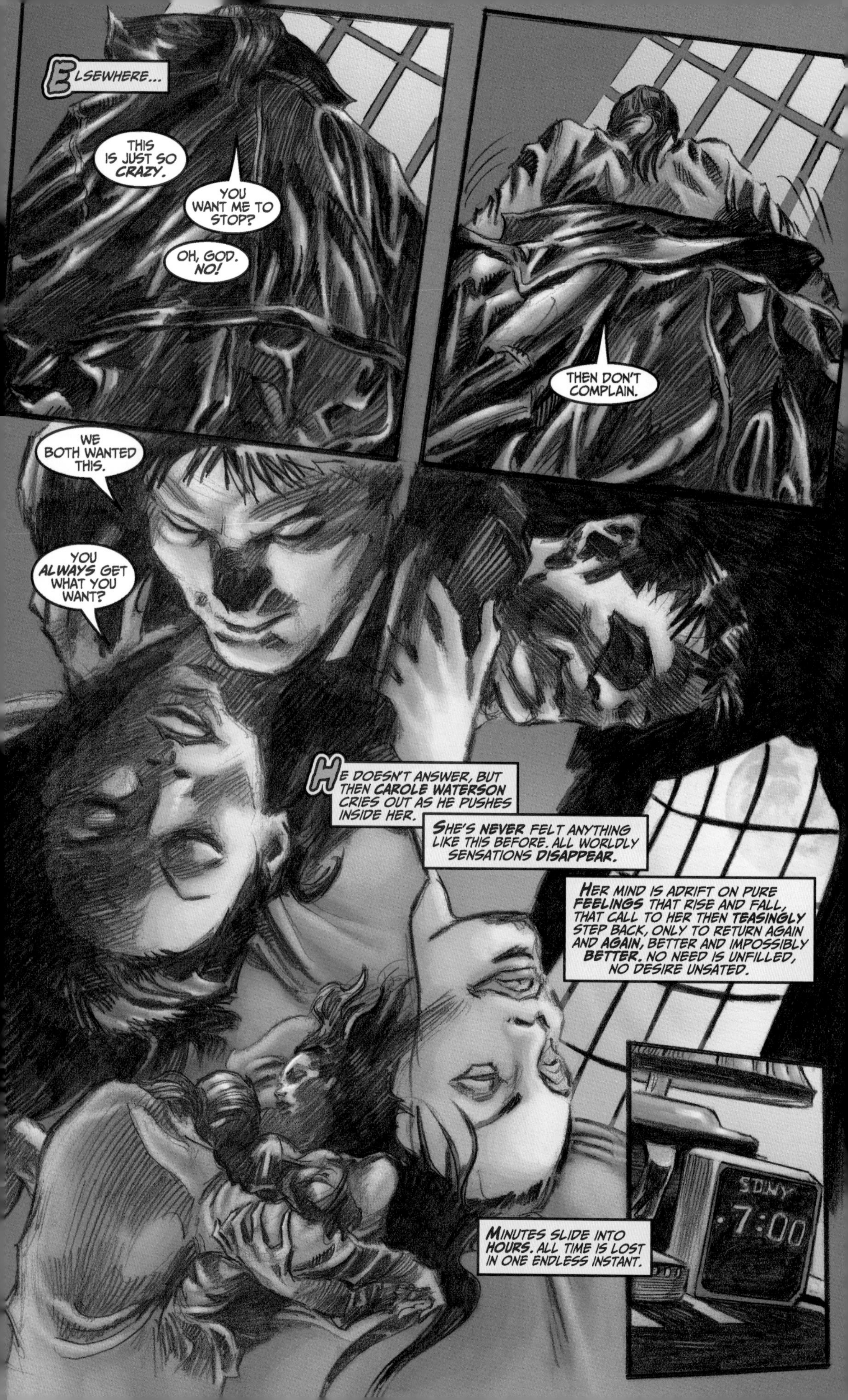
ELSEWHERE...
THIS IS JUST SO CRAZY.
YOU WANT ME TO STOP?
OH, GOD. NO!
THEN DON'T COMPLAIN.
WE BOTH WANTED THIS.
YOU ALWAYS GET WHAT YOU WANT?
HE DOESN'T ANSWER, BUT THEN CAROLE WATERSON CRIES OUT AS HE PUSHES INSIDE HER.
SHE'S NEVER FELT ANYTHING LIKE THIS BEFORE. ALL WORLDLY SENSATIONS DISAPPEAR.
HER MIND IS ADRIFT ON PURE FEELINGS THAT RISE AND FALL, THAT CALL TO HER THEN TEASINGLY STEP BACK, ONLY TO RETURN AGAIN AND AGAIN, BETTER AND IMPOSSIBLY BETTER. NO NEED IS UNFILLED, NO DESIRE UNSATED.
MINUTES SLIDE INTO HOURS. ALL TIME IS LOST IN ONE ENDLESS INSTANT.
SONY
7:00

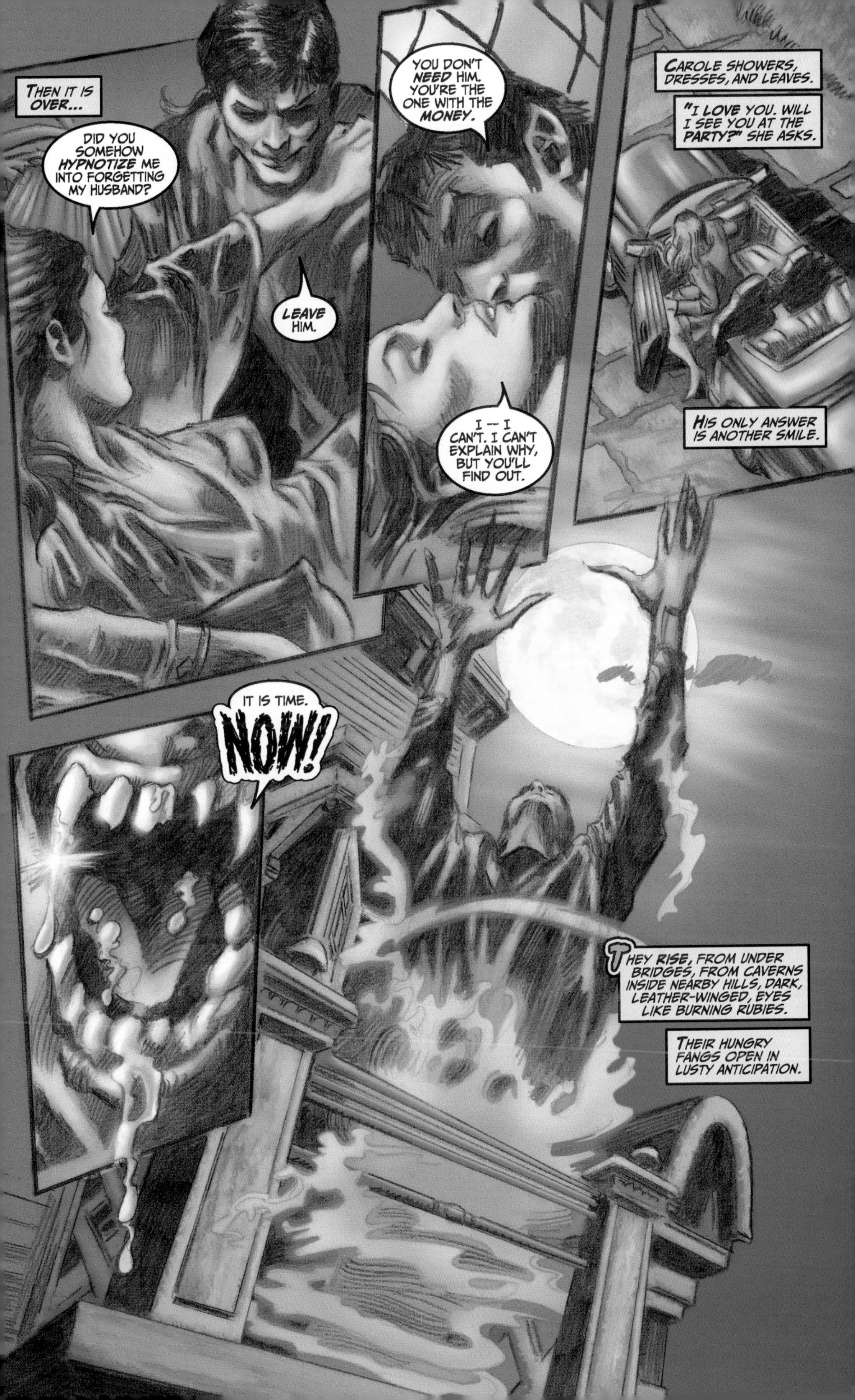

THEN IT IS OVER...
DID YOU SOMEHOW HYPNOTIZE ME INTO FORGETTING MY HUSBAND?
LEAVE HIM.
YOU DON'T NEED HIM. YOU'RE THE ONE WITH THE MONEY.
I -- I CAN'T. I CAN'T EXPLAIN WHY, BUT YOU'LL FIND OUT.
CAROLE SHOWERS, DRESSES, AND LEAVES.
"I LOVE YOU. WILL I SEE YOU AT THE PARTY?" SHE ASKS.
HIS ONLY ANSWER IS ANOTHER SMILE.
IT IS TIME. NOW!
THEY RISE, FROM UNDER BRIDGES, FROM CAVERNS INSIDE NEARBY HILLS, DARK, LEATHER-WINGED, EYES LIKE BURNING RUBIES.
THEIR HUNGRY FANGS OPEN IN LUSTY ANTICIPATION.

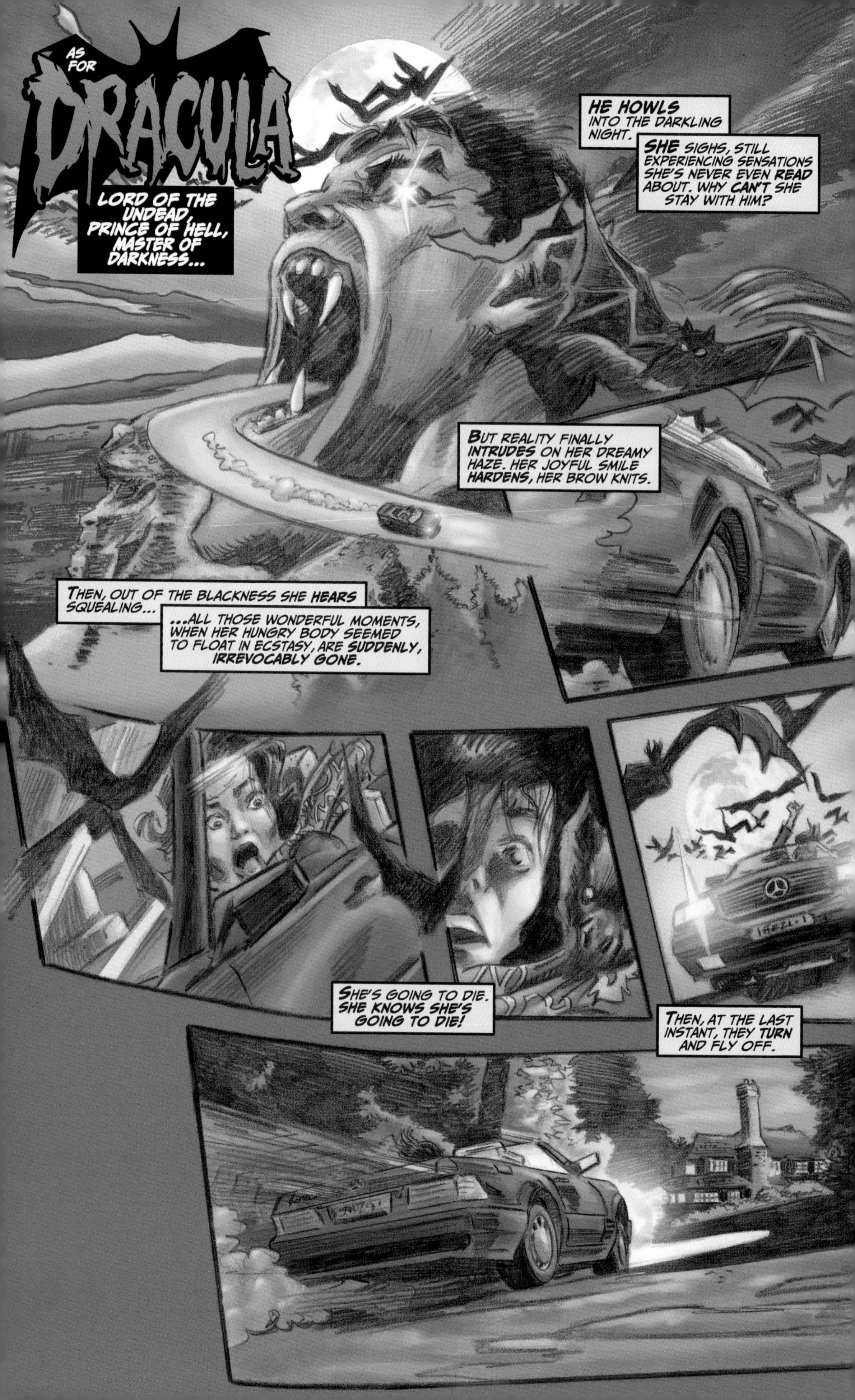
AS FOR
DRACULA
LORD OF THE UNDEAD, PRINCE OF HELL, MASTER OF DARKNESS...
HE HOWLS INTO THE DARKLING NIGHT.
SHE SIGHS, STILL EXPERIENCING SENSATIONS SHE'S NEVER EVEN READ ABOUT. WHY CAN'T SHE STAY WITH HIM?
BUT REALITY FINALLY INTRUDES ON HER DREAMY HAZE. HER JOYFUL SMILE HARDENS, HER BROW KNITS.
THEN, OUT OF THE BLACKNESS SHE HEARS SQUEALING...
...ALL THOSE WONDERFUL MOMENTS, WHEN HER HUNGRY BODY SEEMED TO FLOAT IN ECSTASY, ARE SUDDENLY, IRREVOCABLY GONE.
SHE'S GOING TO DIE. SHE KNOWS SHE'S GOING TO DIE!
THEN, AT THE LAST INSTANT, THEY TURN AND FLY OFF.

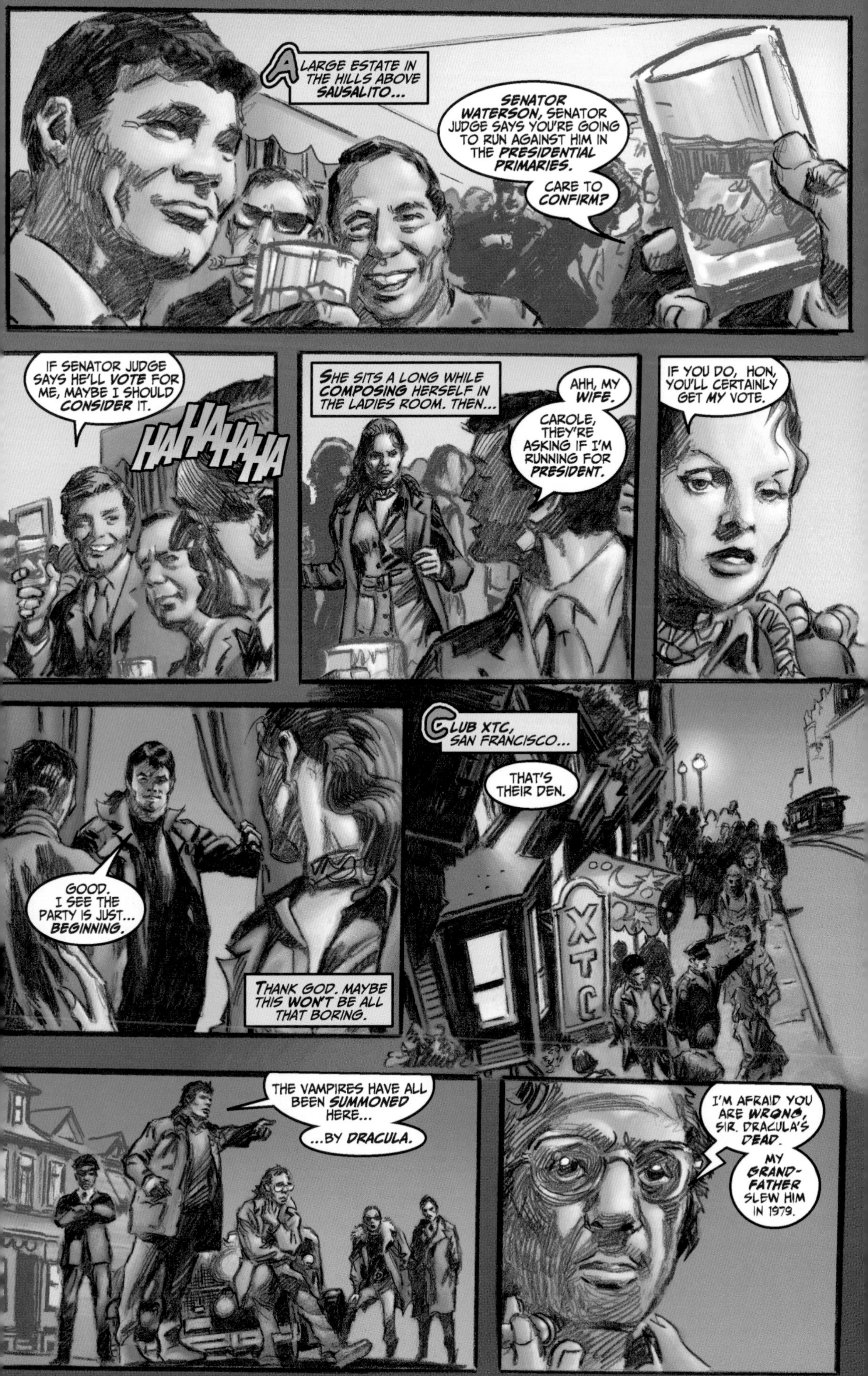
A LARGE ESTATE IN THE HILLS ABOVE SAUSALITO...
SENATOR WATERSON, SENATOR JUDGE SAYS YOU'RE GOING TO RUN AGAINST HIM IN THE PRESIDENTIAL PRIMARIES.
CARE TO CONFIRM?
IF SENATOR JUDGE SAYS HE'LL VOTE FOR ME, MAYBE I SHOULD CONSIDER IT.
HAHAHAHA
SHE SITS A LONG WHILE COMPOSING HERSELF IN THE LADIES ROOM. THEN...
AHH, MY WIFE.
CAROLE, THEY'RE ASKING IF I'M RUNNING FOR PRESIDENT.
IF YOU DO, HON, YOU'LL CERTAINLY GET MY VOTE.
GOOD. I SEE THE PARTY IS JUST... BEGINNING.
THANK GOD. MAYBE THIS WON'T BE ALL THAT BORING.
CLUB XTC, SAN FRANCISCO...
THAT'S THEIR DEN.
XTC
THE VAMPIRES HAVE ALL BEEN SUMMONED HERE...
...BY DRACULA.
I'M AFRAID YOU ARE WRONG, SIR. DRACULA'S DEAD.
MY GRAND-FATHER SLEW HIM IN 1979.

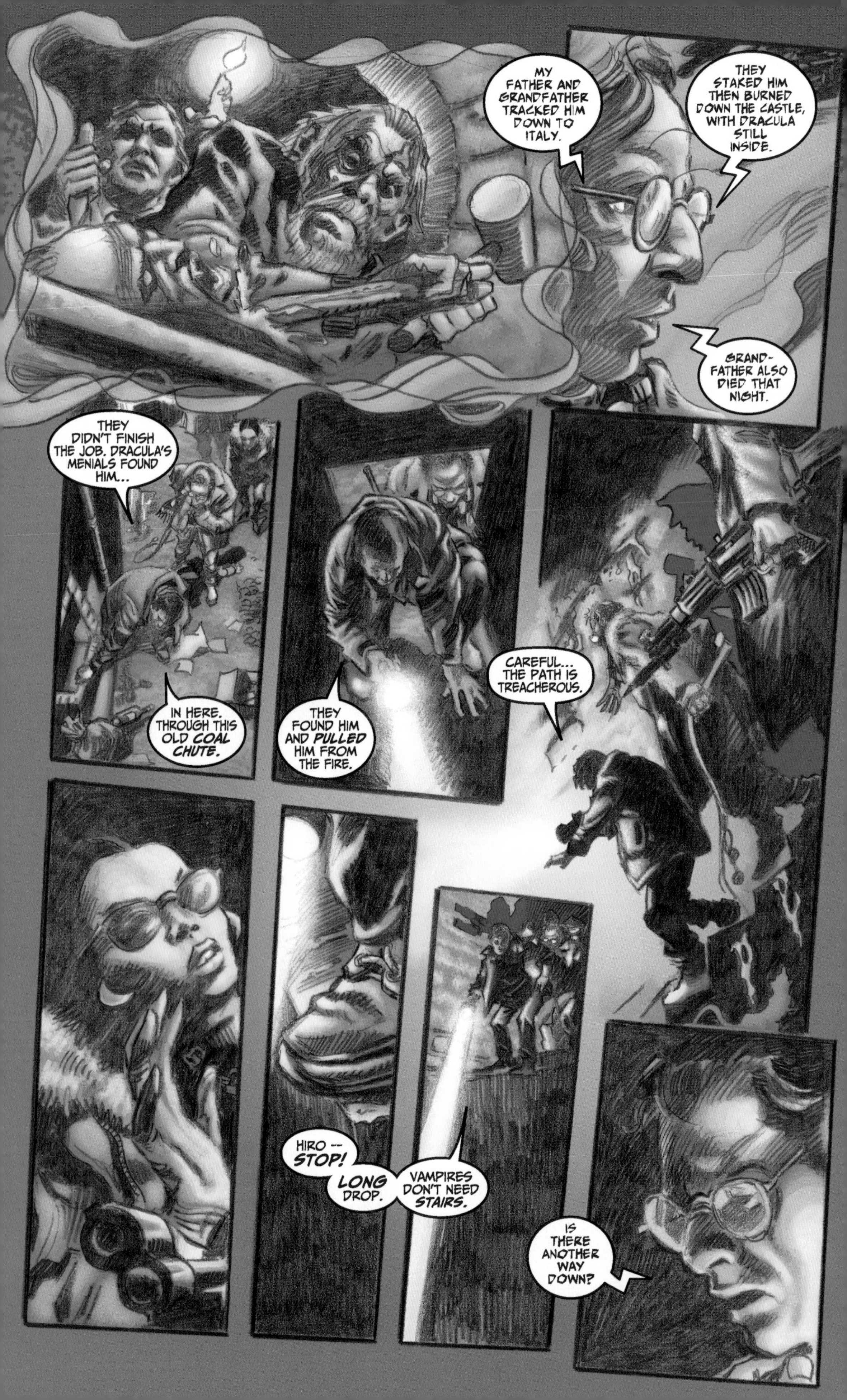
MY FATHER AND GRANDFATHER TRACKED HIM DOWN TO ITALY.
THEY STAKED HIM THEN BURNED DOWN THE CASTLE, WITH DRACULA STILL INSIDE.
GRAND-FATHER ALSO DIED THAT NIGHT.
THEY DIDN'T FINISH THE JOB. DRACULA'S MENIALS FOUND HIM...
IN HERE. THROUGH THIS OLD COAL CHUTE.
THEY FOUND HIM AND PULLED HIM FROM THE FIRE.
CAREFUL... THE PATH IS TREACHEROUS.
HIRO -- STOP!
LONG DROP.
VAMPIRES DON'T NEED STAIRS.
IS THERE ANOTHER WAY DOWN?

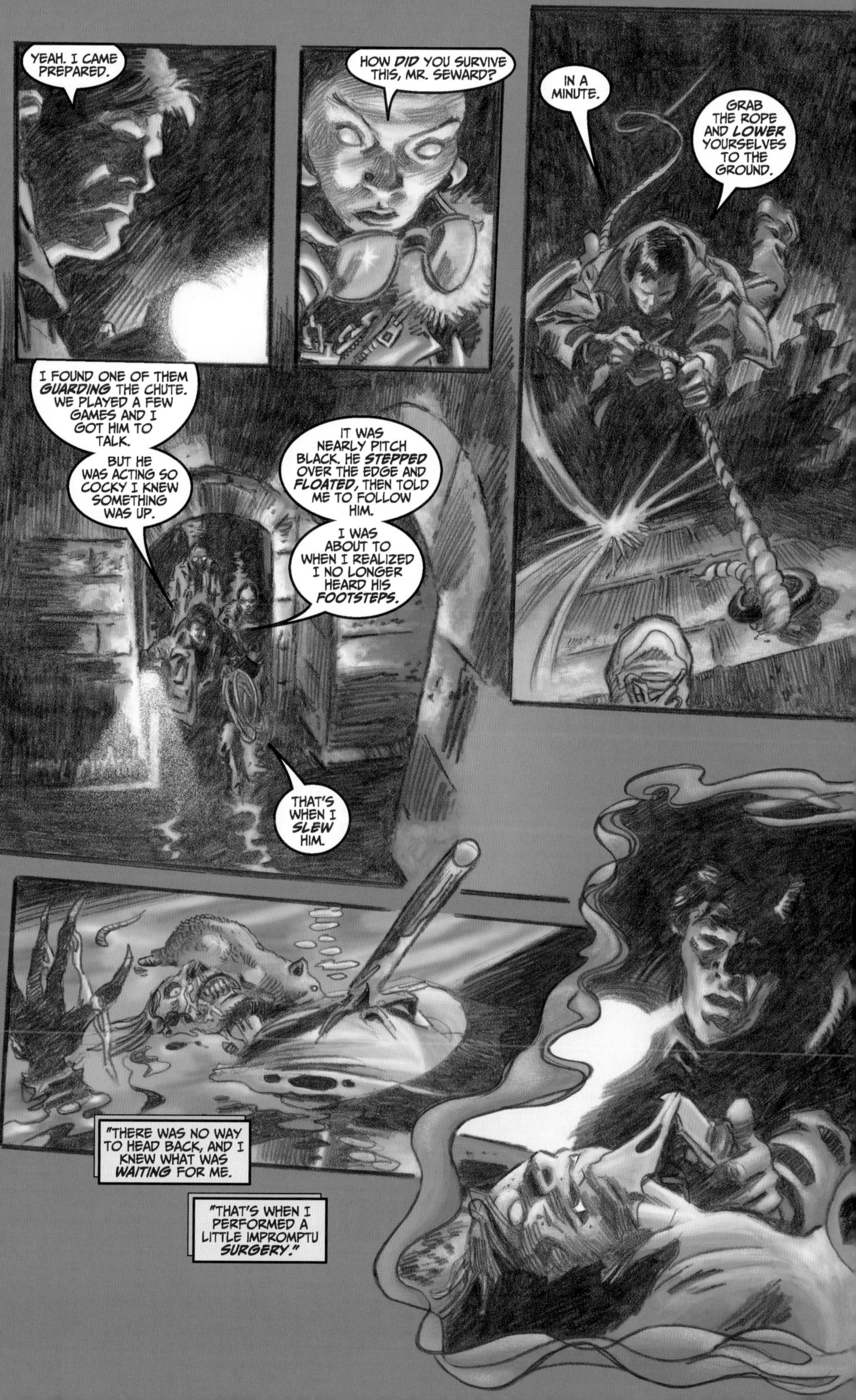
YEAH. I CAME PREPARED.
HOW DID YOU SURVIVE THIS, MR. SEWARD?
IN A MINUTE.
GRAB THE ROPE AND LOWER YOURSELVES TO THE GROUND.
I FOUND ONE OF THEM GUARDING THE CHUTE. WE PLAYED A FEW GAMES AND I GOT HIM TO TALK.
BUT HE WAS ACTING SO COCKY I KNEW SOMETHING WAS UP.
IT WAS NEARLY PITCH BLACK. HE STEPPED OVER THE EDGE AND FLOATED, THEN TOLD ME TO FOLLOW HIM.
I WAS ABOUT TO WHEN I REALIZED I NO LONGER HEARD HIS FOOTSTEPS.
THAT'S WHEN I SLEW HIM.
"THERE WAS NO WAY TO HEAD BACK, AND I KNEW WHAT WAS WAITING FOR ME.
"THAT'S WHEN I PERFORMED A LITTLE IMPROMPTU SURGERY."

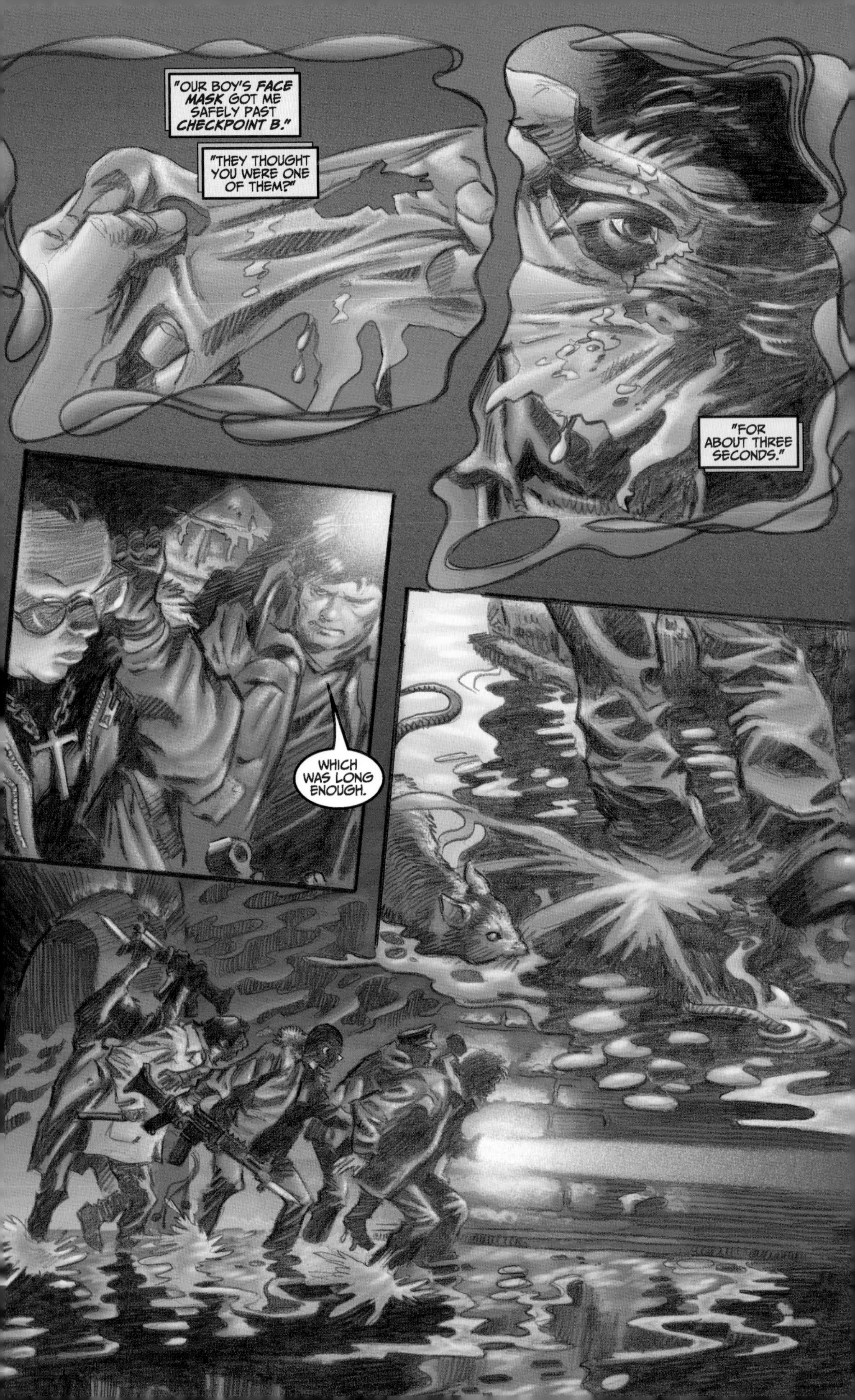
"OUR BOY'S FACE MASK GOT ME SAFELY PAST CHECKPOINT B."
"THEY THOUGHT YOU WERE ONE OF THEM?"
"FOR ABOUT THREE SECONDS."
WHICH WAS LONG ENOUGH.

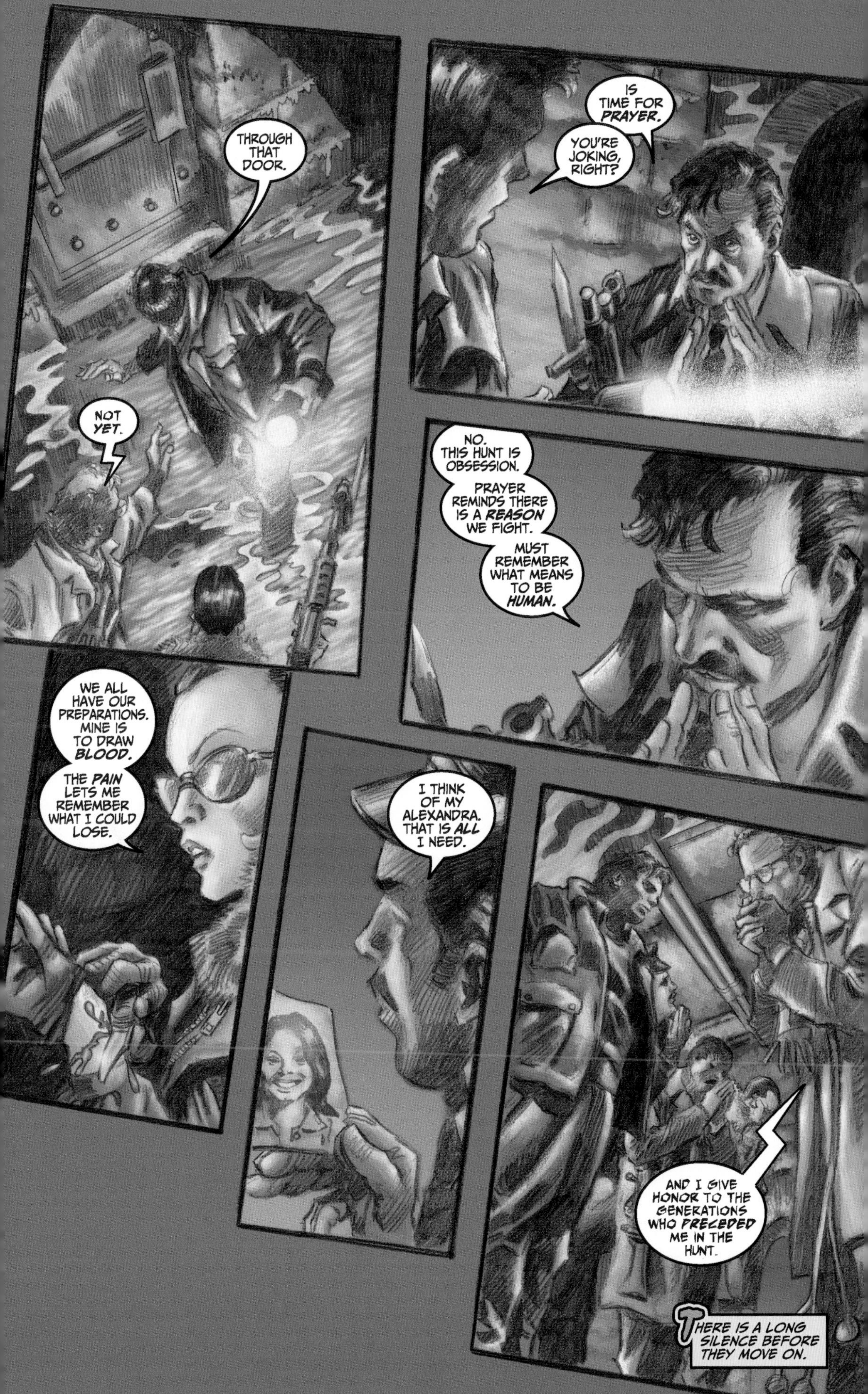
THROUGH THAT DOOR.
NOT YET.
IS TIME FOR PRAYER.
YOU'RE JOKING, RIGHT?
NO. THIS HUNT IS OBSESSION.
PRAYER REMINDS THERE IS A REASON WE FIGHT.
MUST REMEMBER WHAT MEANS TO BE HUMAN.
WE ALL HAVE OUR PREPARATIONS. MINE IS TO DRAW BLOOD.
THE PAIN LETS ME REMEMBER WHAT I COULD LOSE.
I THINK OF MY ALEXANDRA. THAT IS ALL I NEED.
AND I GIVE HONOR TO THE GENERATIONS WHO PRECEDED ME IN THE HUNT.
THERE IS A LONG SILENCE BEFORE THEY MOVE ON.

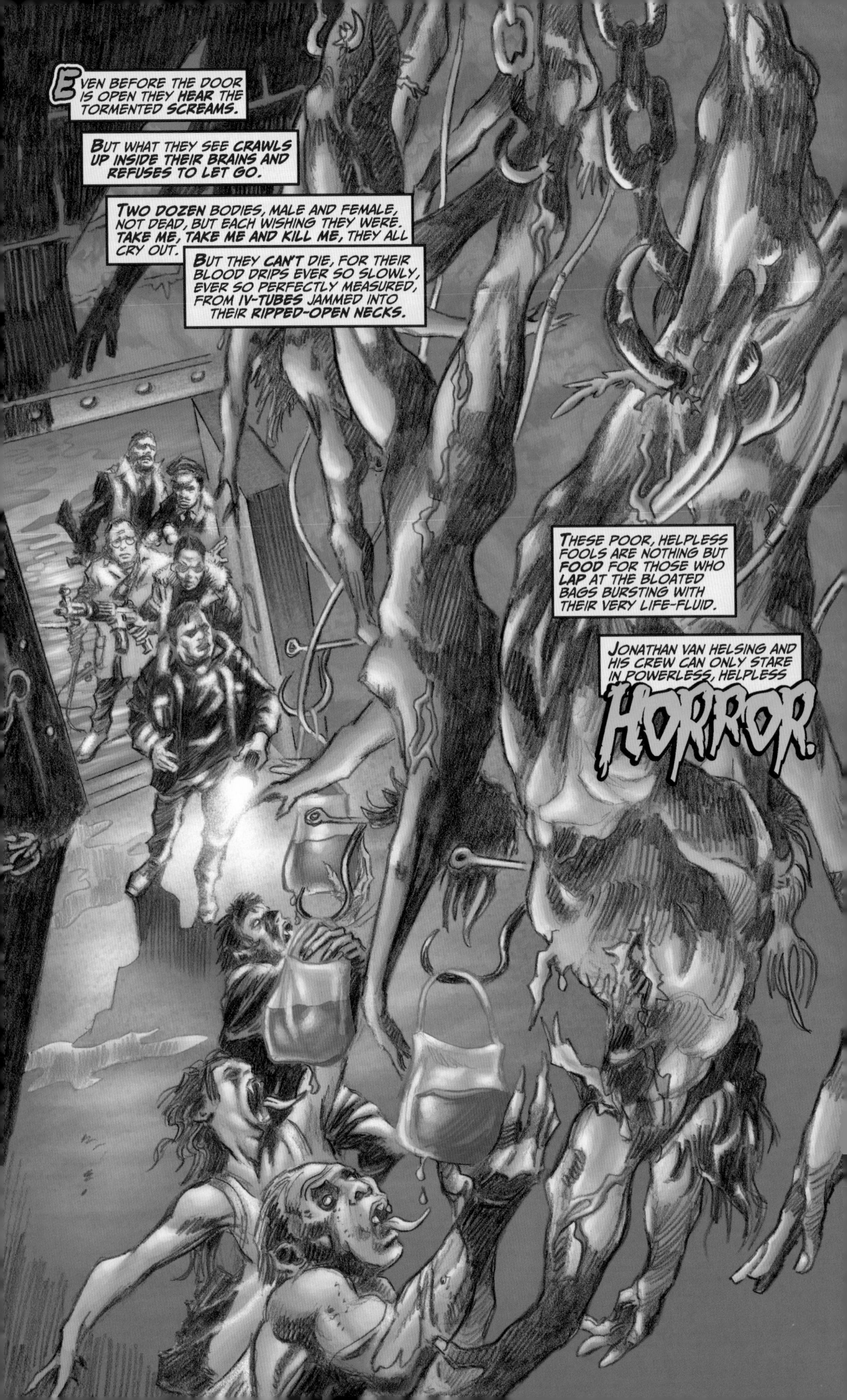
EVEN BEFORE THE DOOR IS OPEN THEY HEAR THE TORMENTED SCREAMS.
BUT WHAT THEY SEE CRAWLS UP INSIDE THEIR BRAINS AND REFUSES TO LET GO.
TWO DOZEN BODIES, MALE AND FEMALE, NOT DEAD, BUT EACH WISHING THEY WERE. TAKE ME, TAKE ME AND KILL ME, THEY ALL CRY OUT.
BUT THEY CAN'T DIE, FOR THEIR BLOOD DRIPS EVER SO SLOWLY, EVER SO PERFECTLY MEASURED, FROM IV-TUBES JAMMED INTO THEIR RIPPED-OPEN NECKS.
THESE POOR, HELPLESS FOOLS ARE NOTHING BUT FOOD FOR THOSE WHO LAP AT THE BLOATED BAGS BURSTING WITH THEIR VERY LIFE-FLUID.
JONATHAN VAN HELSING AND HIS CREW CAN ONLY STARE IN POWERLESS, HELPLESS
HORROR.

Chapter II

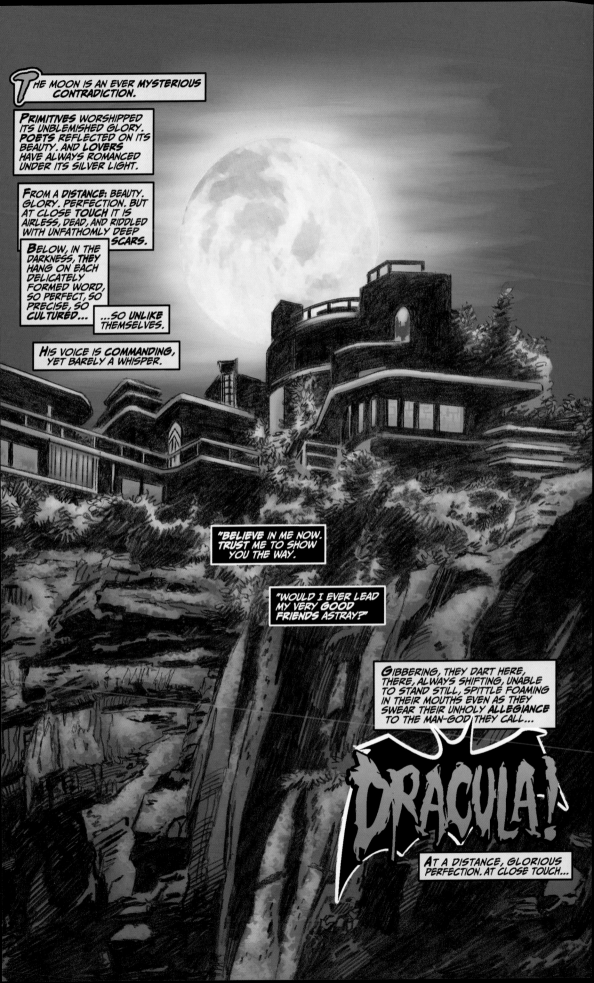

THE MOON IS AN EVER MYSTERIOUS CONTRADICTION.

PRIMITIVES WORSHIPPED ITS UNBLEMISHED GLORY. POETS REFLECTED ON ITS BEAUTY. AND LOVERS HAVE ALWAYS ROMANCED UNDER ITS SILVER LIGHT.

FROM A DISTANCE: BEAUTY. GLORY. PERFECTION. BUT AT CLOSE TOUCH IT IS AIRLESS, DEAD, AND RIDDLED WITH UNFATHOMLY DEEP SCARS.

BELOW, IN THE DARKNESS, THEY HANG ON EACH DELICATELY FORMED WORD, SO PERFECT, SO PRECISE, SO CULTURED...

...SO UNLIKE THEMSELVES.

HIS VOICE IS COMMANDING, YET BARELY A WHISPER.

"BELIEVE IN ME NOW. TRUST ME TO SHOW YOU THE WAY."

"WOULD I EVER LEAD MY VERY GOOD FRIENDS ASTRAY?"

GIBBERING, THEY DART HERE, THERE, ALWAYS SHIFTING, UNABLE TO STAND STILL, SPITTLE FOAMING IN THEIR MOUTHS EVEN AS THEY SWEAR THEIR UNHOLY ALLEGIANCE TO THE MAN-GOD THEY CALL...

DRACULA!

AT A DISTANCE, GLORIOUS PERFECTION. AT CLOSE TOUCH...

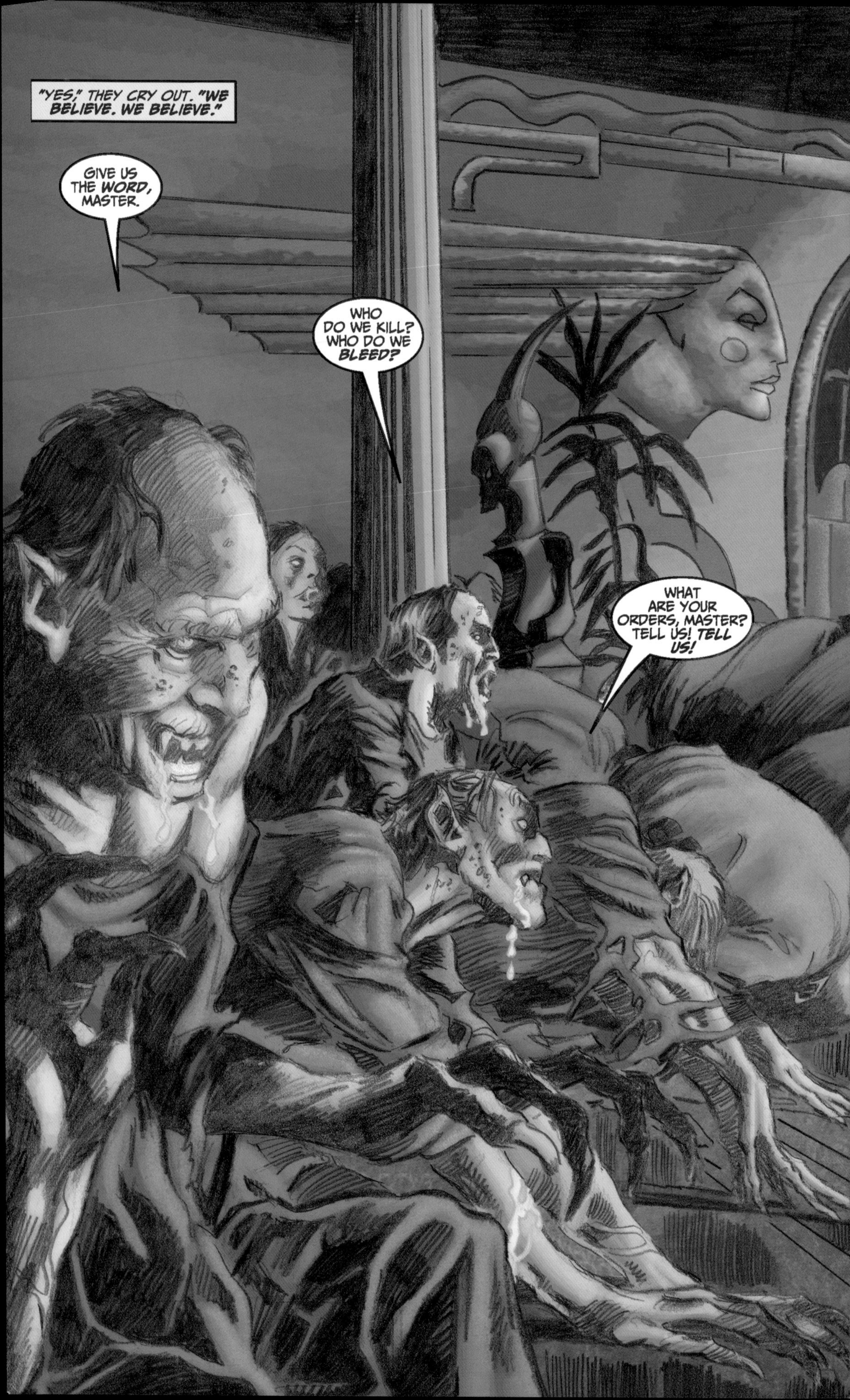
"YES," THEY CRY OUT. "WE BELIEVE. WE BELIEVE."
GIVE US THE WORD, MASTER.
WHO DO WE KILL? WHO DO WE BLEED?
WHAT ARE YOUR ORDERS, MASTER? TELL US! TELL US!

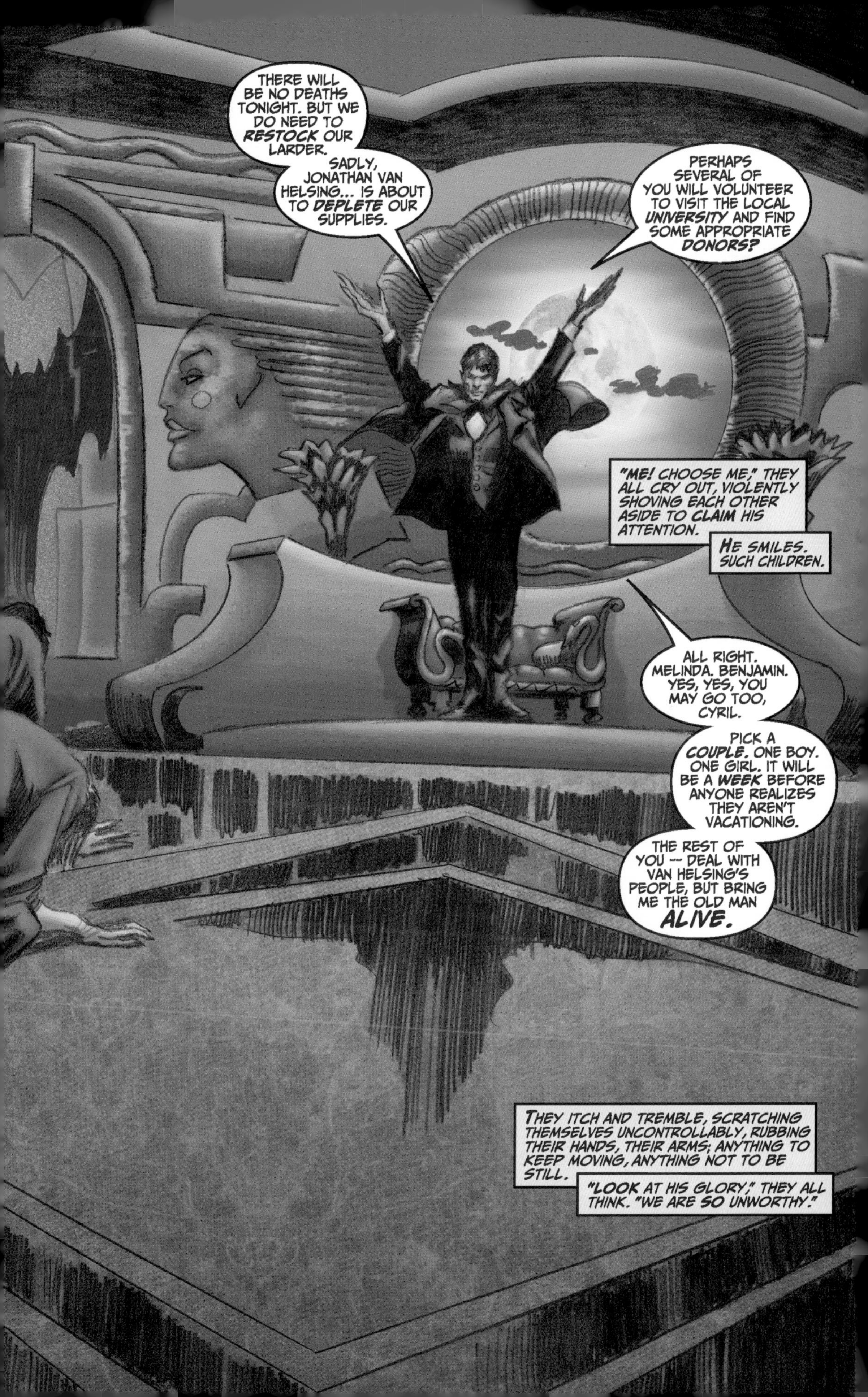
THERE WILL BE NO DEATHS TONIGHT. BUT WE DO NEED TO RESTOCK OUR LARDER.
SADLY, JONATHAN VAN HELSING... IS ABOUT TO DEPLETE OUR SUPPLIES.
PERHAPS SEVERAL OF YOU WILL VOLUNTEER TO VISIT THE LOCAL UNIVERSITY AND FIND SOME APPROPRIATE DONORS?
"ME! CHOOSE ME," THEY ALL CRY OUT, VIOLENTLY SHOVING EACH OTHER ASIDE TO CLAIM HIS ATTENTION.
HE SMILES. SUCH CHILDREN.
ALL RIGHT. MELINDA. BENJAMIN. YES, YES, YOU MAY GO TOO, CYRIL.
PICK A COUPLE. ONE BOY. ONE GIRL. IT WILL BE A WEEK BEFORE ANYONE REALIZES THEY AREN'T VACATIONING.
THE REST OF YOU -- DEAL WITH VAN HELSING'S PEOPLE, BUT BRING ME THE OLD MAN ALIVE.
THEY ITCH AND TREMBLE, SCRATCHING THEMSELVES UNCONTROLLABLY, RUBBING THEIR HANDS, THEIR ARMS; ANYTHING TO KEEP MOVING, ANYTHING NOT TO BE STILL.
"LOOK AT HIS GLORY," THEY ALL THINK. "WE ARE SO UNWORTHY."

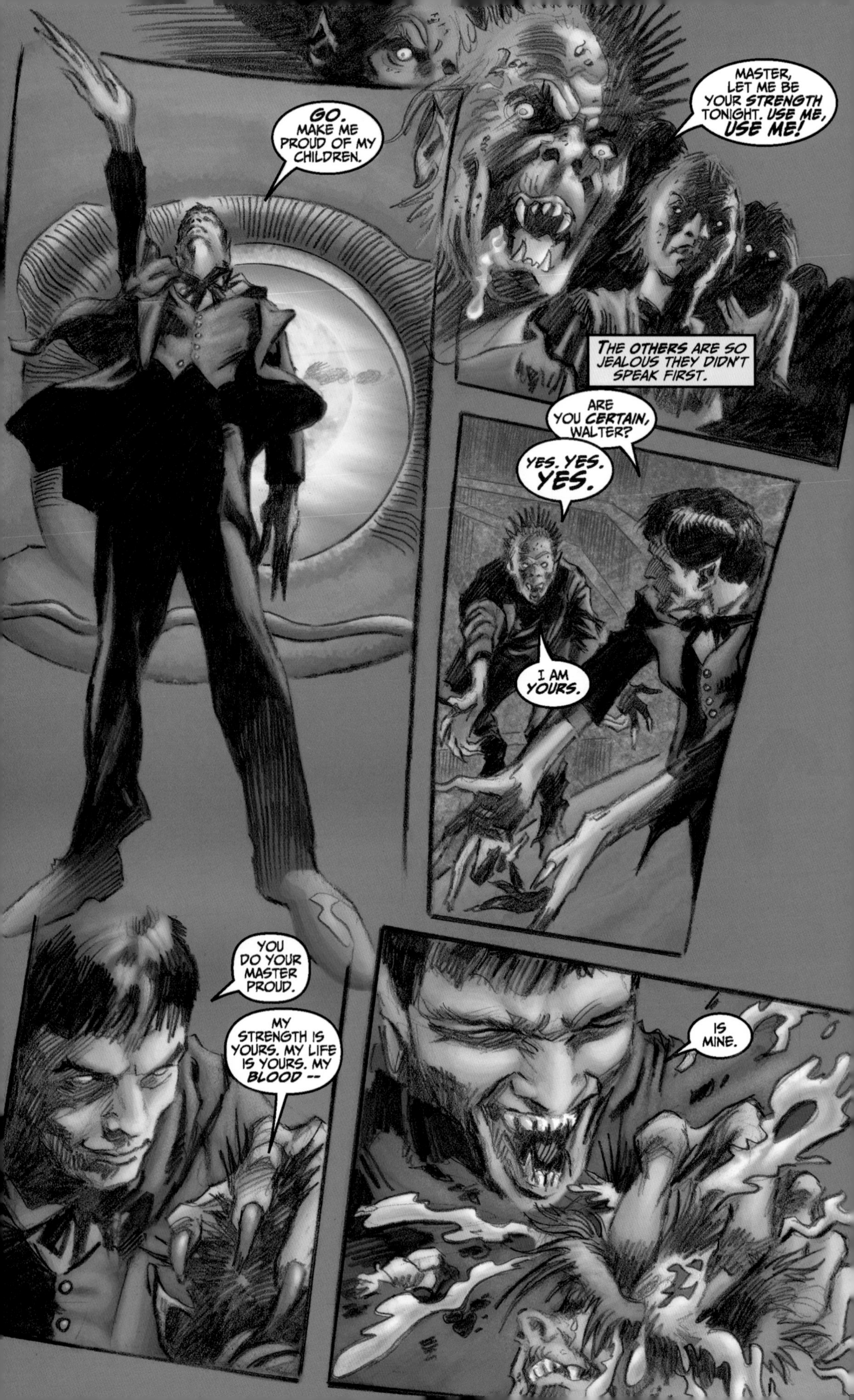
GO. MAKE ME PROUD OF MY CHILDREN.
MASTER, LET ME BE YOUR STRENGTH TONIGHT. USE ME, USE ME!
THE OTHERS ARE SO JEALOUS THEY DIDN'T SPEAK FIRST.
ARE YOU CERTAIN, WALTER?
YES. YES. YES.
I AM YOURS.
YOU DO YOUR MASTER PROUD.
MY STRENGTH IS YOURS. MY LIFE IS YOURS. MY BLOOD --
IS MINE.

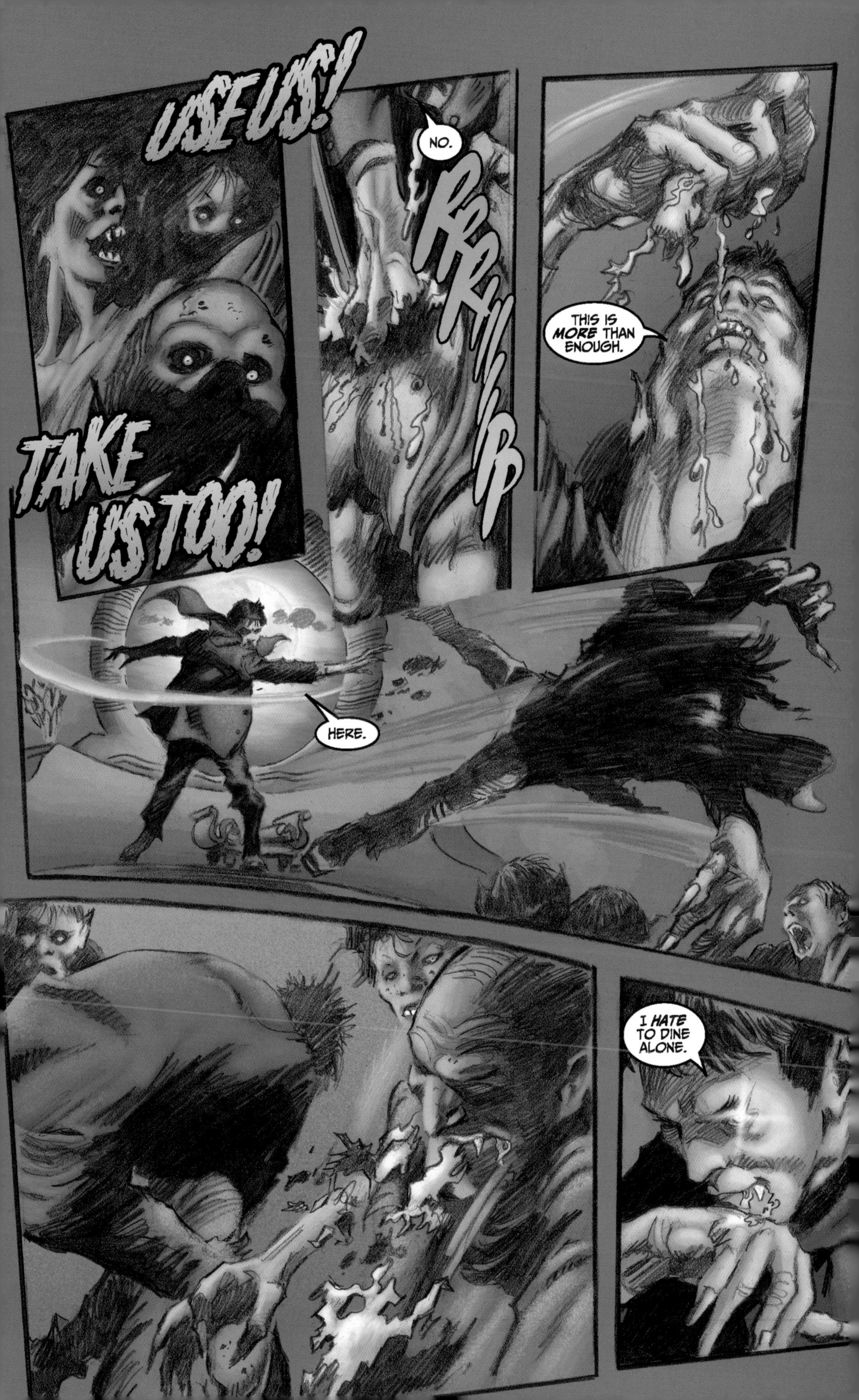
USE US!
TAKE US TOO!
NO.
RRRRIIIIIP
THIS IS MORE THAN ENOUGH.
HERE.
I HATE TO DINE ALONE.

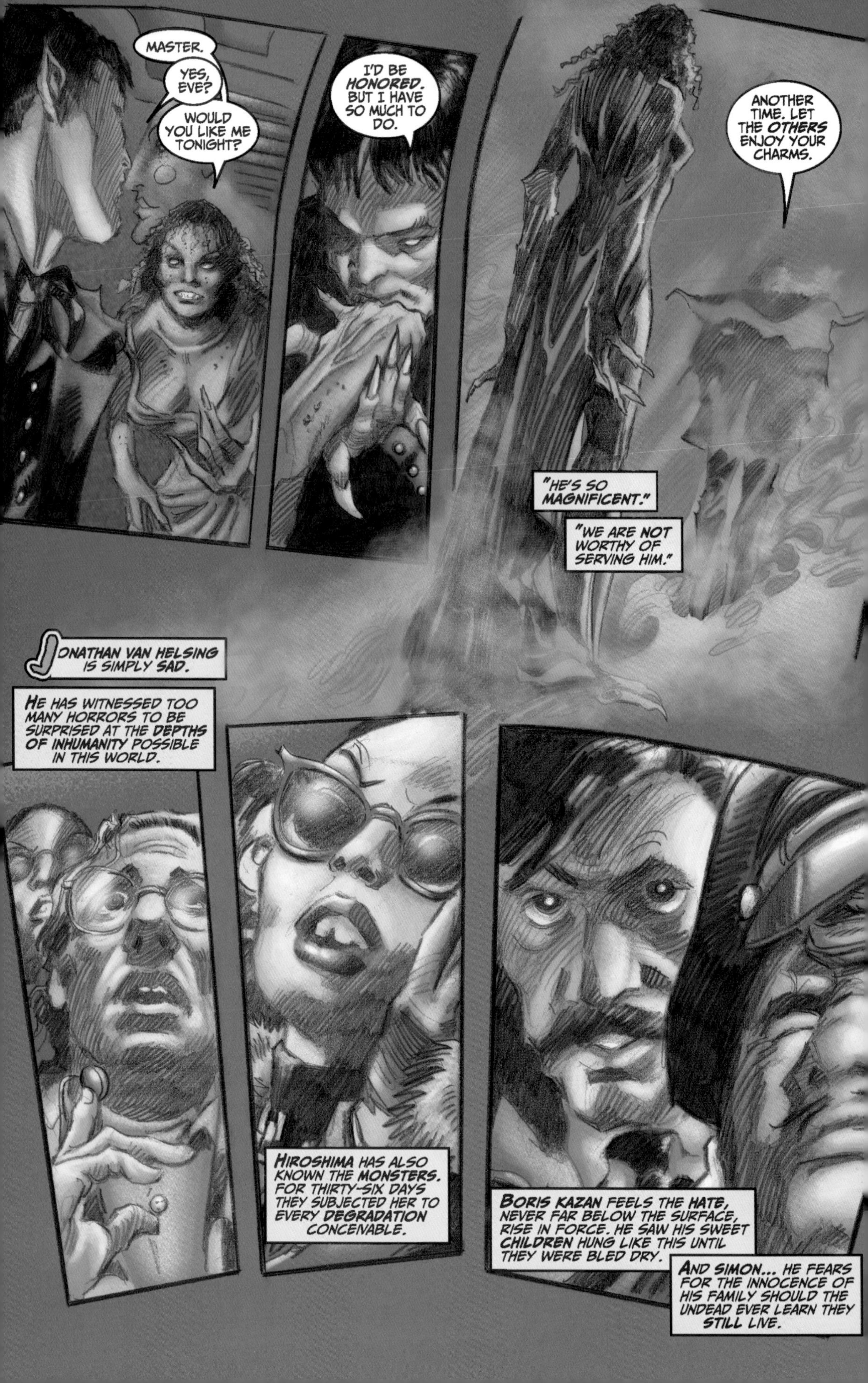
MASTER.
YES, EVE?
WOULD YOU LIKE ME TONIGHT?
I'D BE HONORED. BUT I HAVE SO MUCH TO DO.
ANOTHER TIME. LET THE OTHERS ENJOY YOUR CHARMS.
"HE'S SO MAGNIFICENT."
"WE ARE NOT WORTHY OF SERVING HIM."
JONATHAN VAN HELSING IS SIMPLY SAD.
HE HAS WITNESSED TOO MANY HORRORS TO BE SURPRISED AT THE DEPTHS OF INHUMANITY POSSIBLE IN THIS WORLD.
HIROSHIMA HAS ALSO KNOWN THE MONSTERS. FOR THIRTY-SIX DAYS THEY SUBJECTED HER TO EVERY DEGRADATION CONCEIVABLE.
BORIS KAZAN FEELS THE HATE, NEVER FAR BELOW THE SURFACE, RISE IN FORCE. HE SAW HIS SWEET CHILDREN HUNG LIKE THIS UNTIL THEY WERE BLED DRY.
AND SIMON... HE FEARS FOR THE INNOCENCE OF HIS FAMILY SHOULD THE UNDEAD EVER LEARN THEY STILL LIVE.

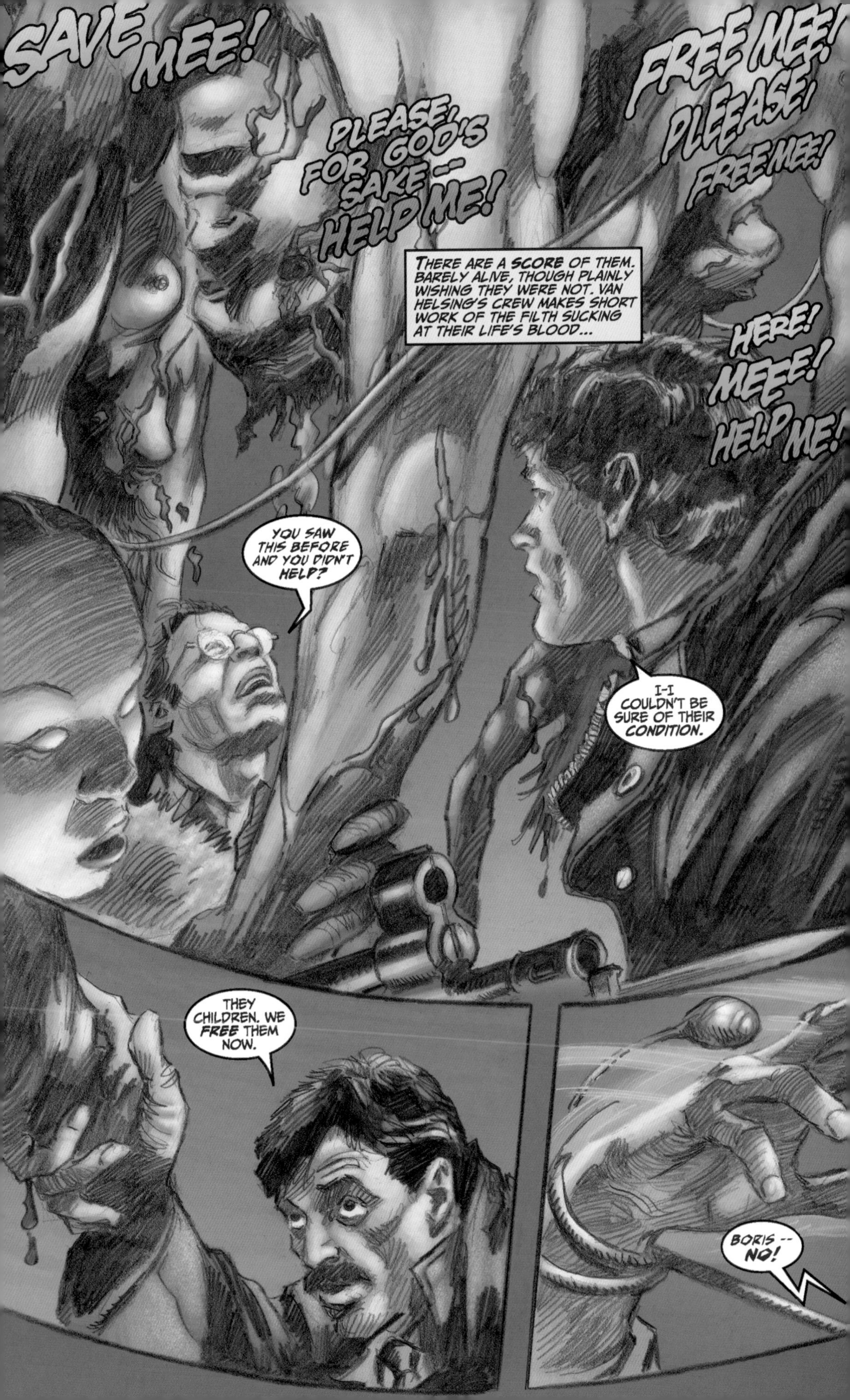
SAVE MEE!
PLEASE, FOR GOD'S SAKE -- HELP ME!
FREE MEE! PLEEASE! FREE MEE!
THERE ARE A SCORE OF THEM. BARELY ALIVE, THOUGH PLAINLY WISHING THEY WERE NOT. VAN HELSING'S CREW MAKES SHORT WORK OF THE FILTH SUCKING AT THEIR LIFE'S BLOOD...
HERE! MEEE! HELP ME!
YOU SAW THIS BEFORE AND YOU DIDN'T HELP?
I-I COULDN'T BE SURE OF THEIR CONDITION.
THEY CHILDREN. WE FREE THEM NOW.
BORIS -- NO!

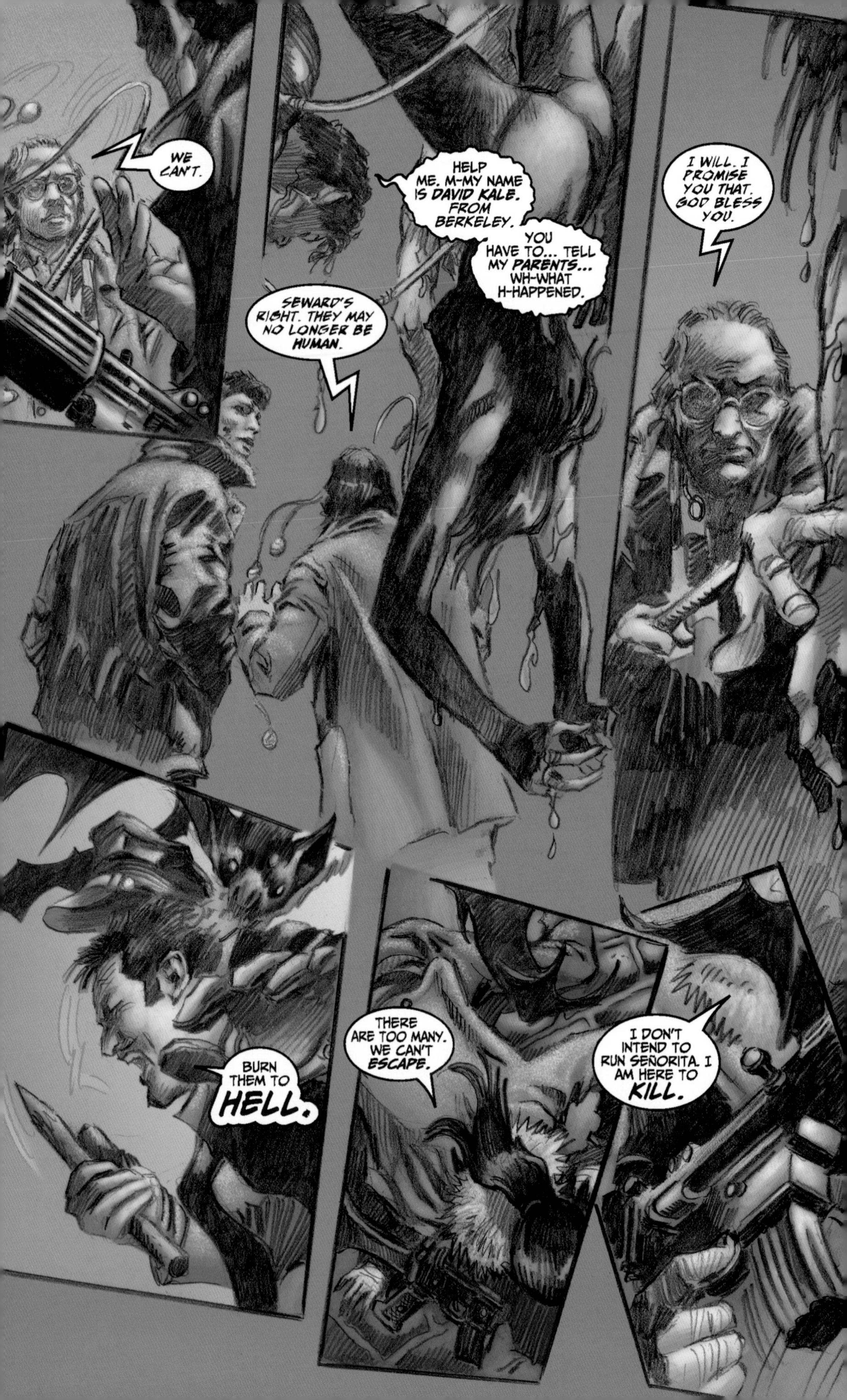
WE CAN'T.
HELP ME. M-MY NAME IS DAVID KALE. FROM BERKELEY.
YOU HAVE TO... TELL MY PARENTS... WH-WHAT H-HAPPENED.
SEWARD'S RIGHT. THEY MAY NO LONGER BE HUMAN.
I WILL. I PROMISE YOU THAT. GOD BLESS YOU.
BURN THEM TO HELL.
THERE ARE TOO MANY. WE CAN'T ESCAPE.
I DON'T INTEND TO RUN SEÑORITA. I AM HERE TO KILL.

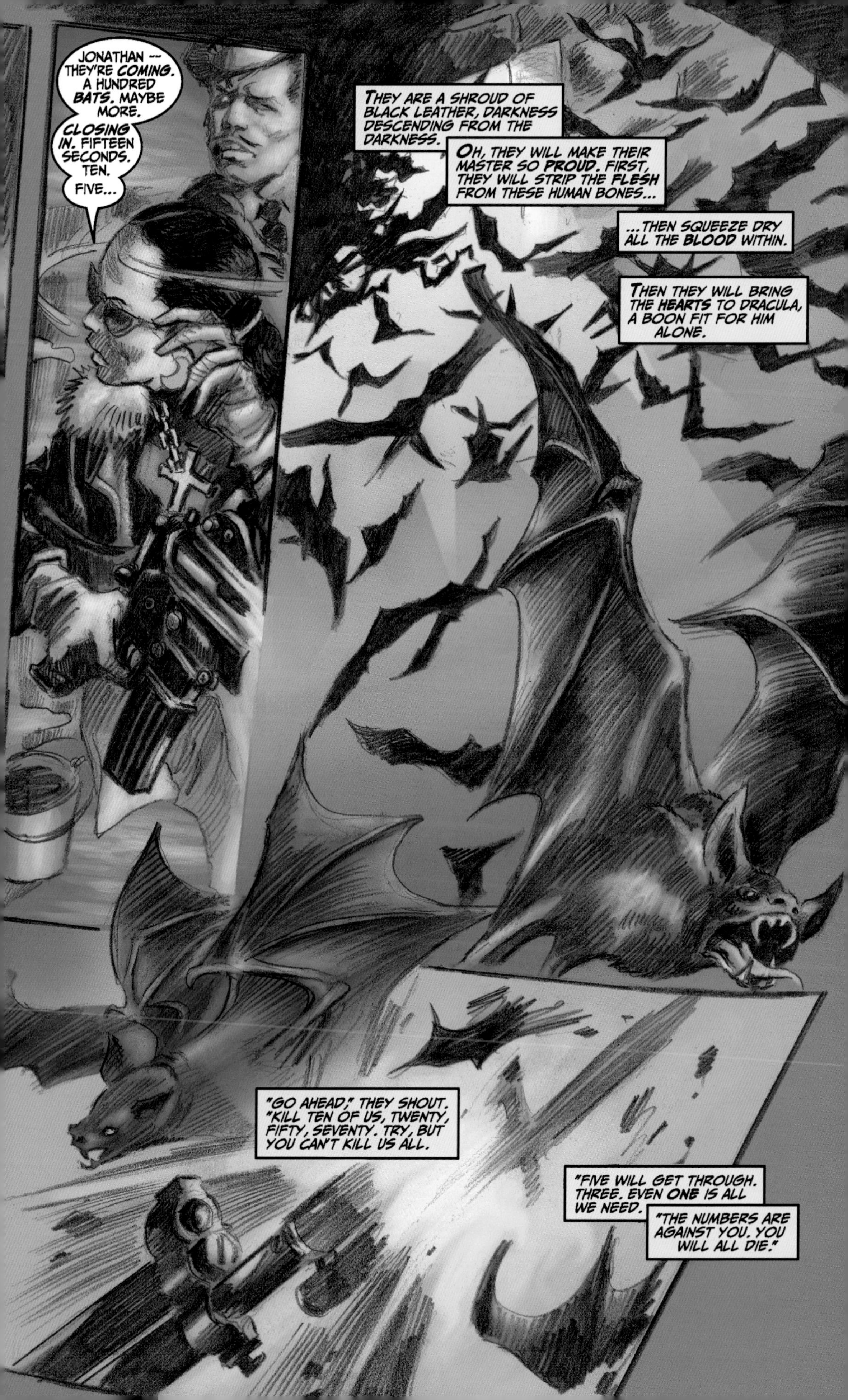
JONATHAN -- THEY'RE COMING. A HUNDRED BATS. MAYBE MORE.
CLOSING IN. FIFTEEN SECONDS. TEN. FIVE...
THEY ARE A SHROUD OF BLACK LEATHER, DARKNESS DESCENDING FROM THE DARKNESS.
OH, THEY WILL MAKE THEIR MASTER SO PROUD. FIRST, THEY WILL STRIP THE FLESH FROM THESE HUMAN BONES...
...THEN SQUEEZE DRY ALL THE BLOOD WITHIN.
THEN THEY WILL BRING THE HEARTS TO DRACULA, A BOON FIT FOR HIM ALONE.
"GO AHEAD," THEY SHOUT. "KILL TEN OF US, TWENTY, FIFTY, SEVENTY. TRY, BUT YOU CAN'T KILL US ALL.
"FIVE WILL GET THROUGH. THREE. EVEN ONE IS ALL WE NEED.
"THE NUMBERS ARE AGAINST YOU. YOU WILL ALL DIE."

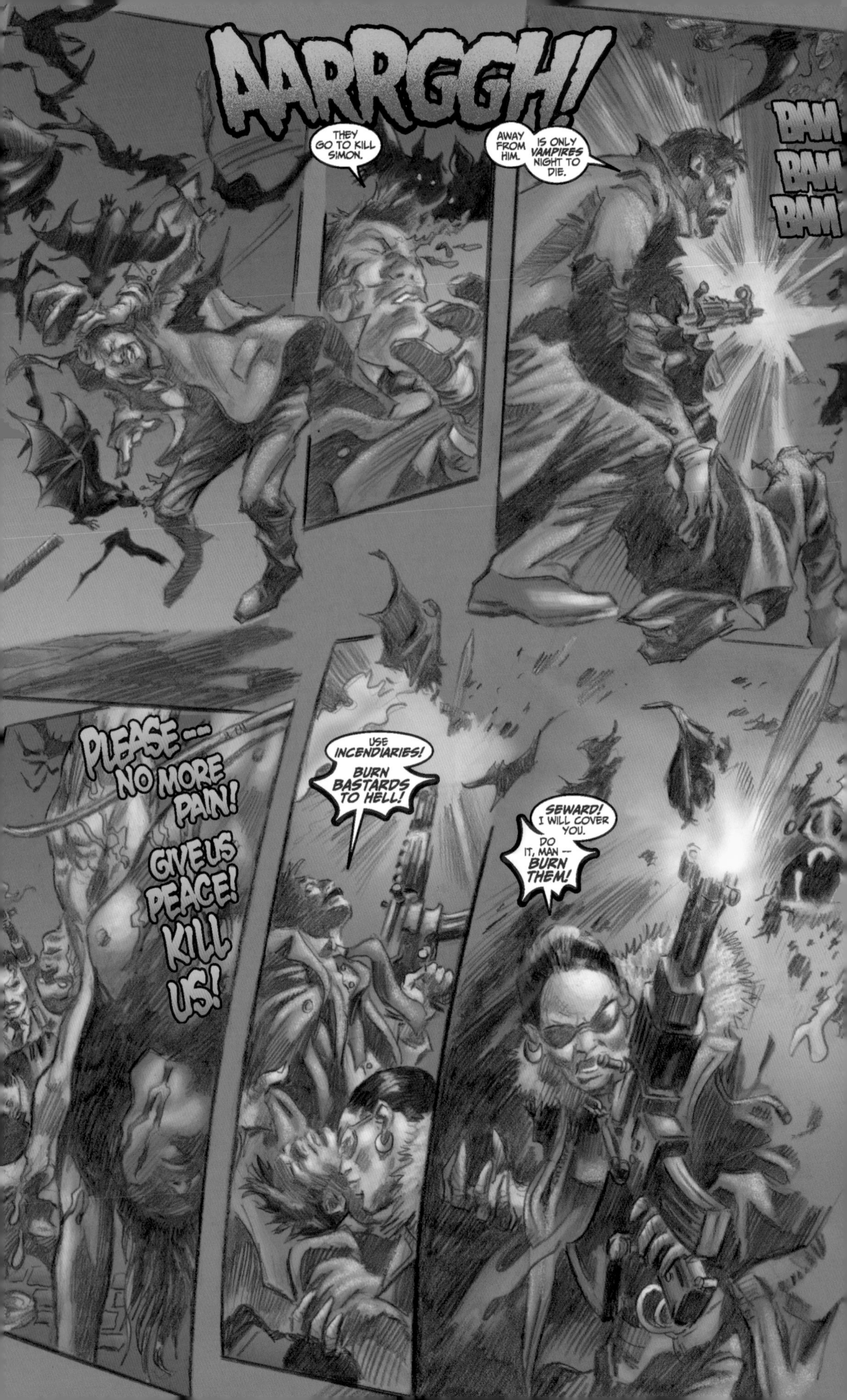
AARRGGH!
THEY GO TO KILL SIMON.
AWAY FROM HIM.
IS ONLY VAMPIRES NIGHT TO DIE.
BAM BAM BAM
PLEASE -- NO MORE PAIN!
GIVE US PEACE! KILL US!
USE INCENDIARIES!
BURN BASTARDS TO HELL!
SEWARD! I WILL COVER YOU.
DO IT, MAN -- BURN THEM!

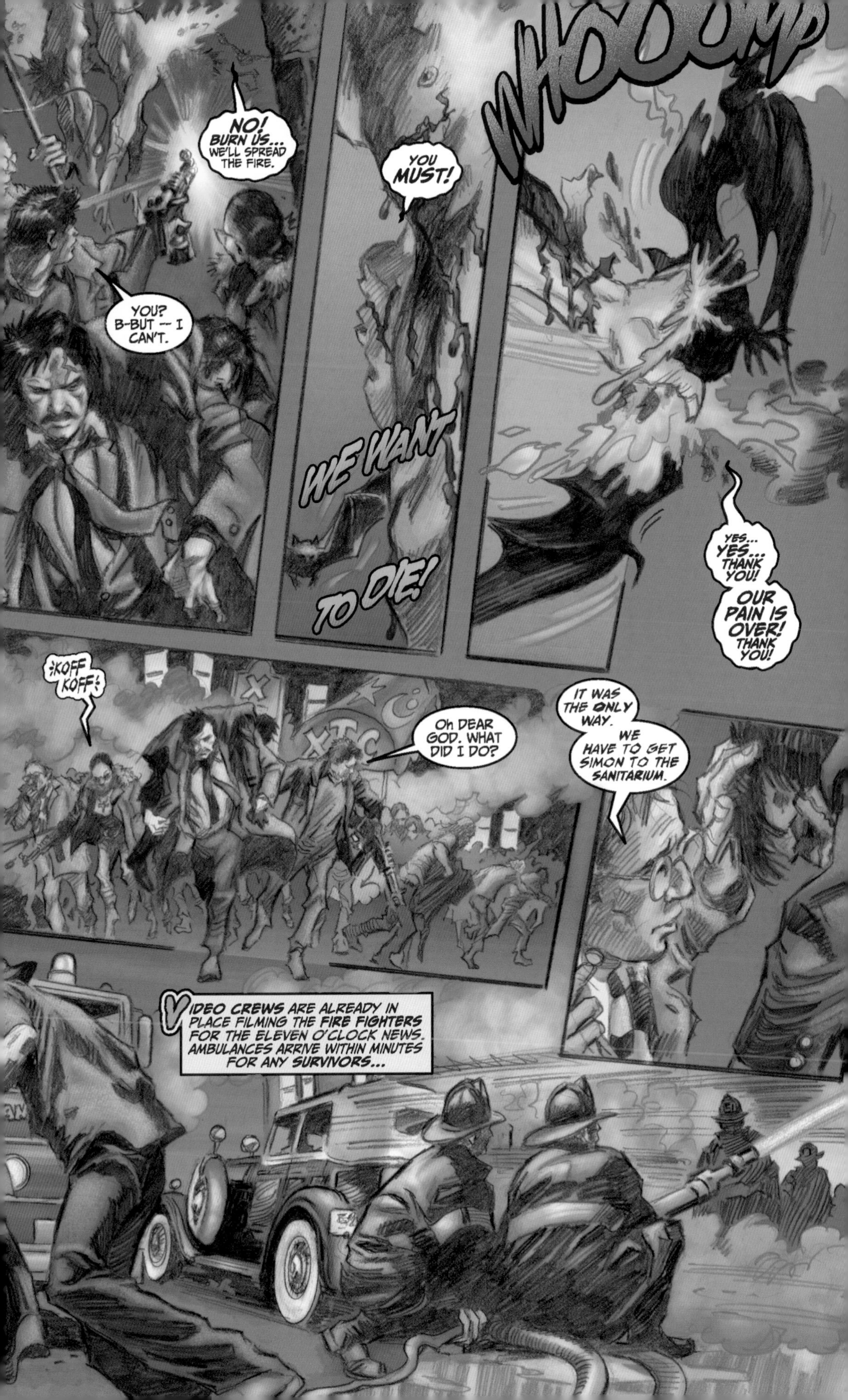
NO! BURN US... WE'LL SPREAD THE FIRE.
YOU? B-BUT -- I CAN'T.
YOU MUST!
WE WANT TO DIE!
WHOOOMP
YES... YES... THANK YOU!
OUR PAIN IS OVER! THANK YOU!
KOFF KOFF
Oh DEAR GOD. WHAT DID I DO?
IT WAS THE ONLY WAY.
WE HAVE TO GET SIMON TO THE SANITARIUM.
VIDEO CREWS ARE ALREADY IN PLACE FILMING THE FIRE FIGHTERS FOR THE ELEVEN O'CLOCK NEWS. AMBULANCES ARRIVE WITHIN MINUTES FOR ANY SURVIVORS...

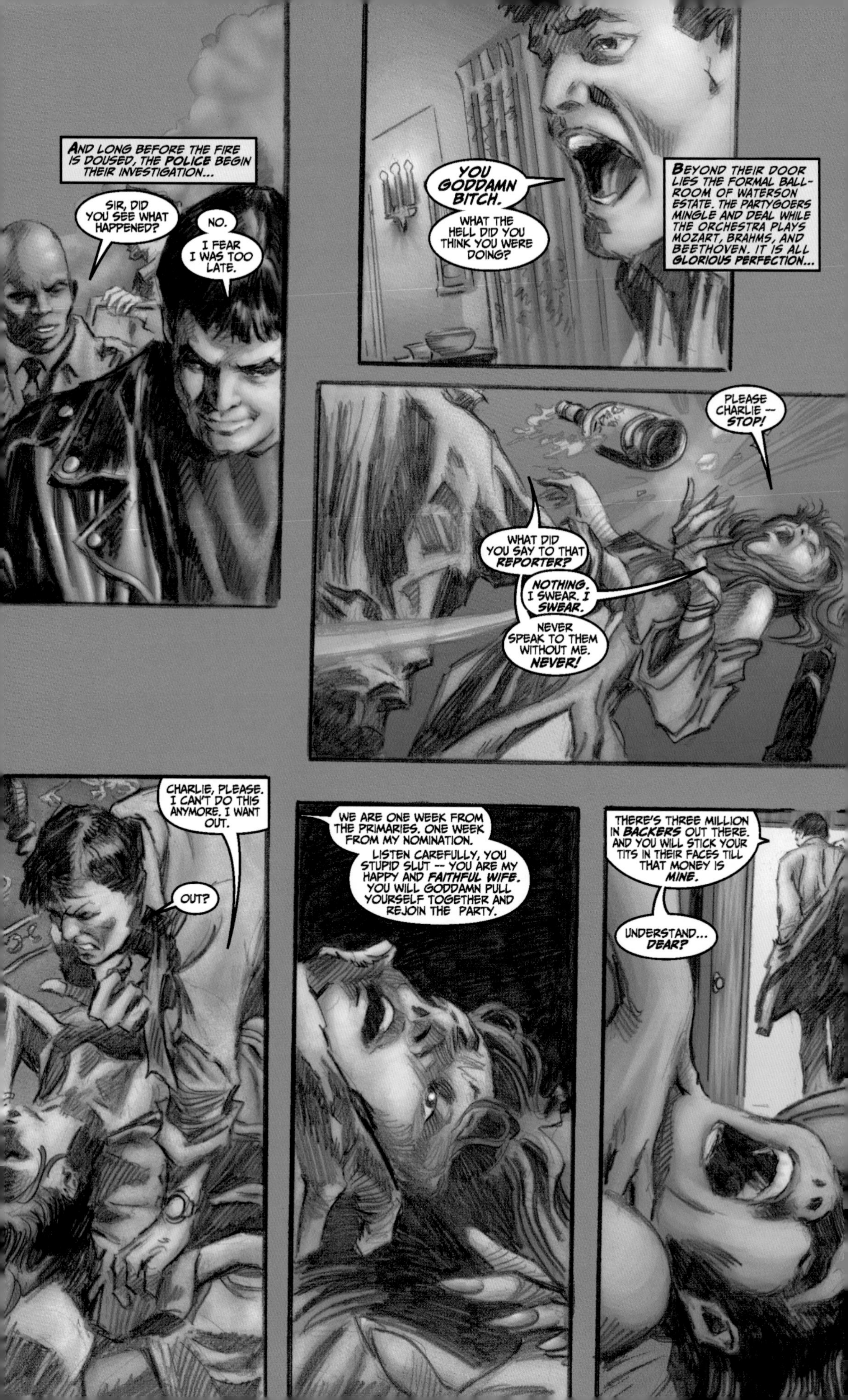

AND LONG BEFORE THE FIRE IS DOUSED, THE POLICE BEGIN THEIR INVESTIGATION...
SIR, DID YOU SEE WHAT HAPPENED?
NO.
I FEAR I WAS TOO LATE.
YOU GODDAMN BITCH.
WHAT THE HELL DID YOU THINK YOU WERE DOING?
BEYOND THEIR DOOR LIES THE FORMAL BALL-ROOM OF WATERSON ESTATE. THE PARTYGOERS MINGLE AND DEAL WHILE THE ORCHESTRA PLAYS MOZART, BRAHMS, AND BEETHOVEN. IT IS ALL GLORIOUS PERFECTION...
PLEASE CHARLIE -- STOP!
WHAT DID YOU SAY TO THAT REPORTER?
NOTHING. I SWEAR. I SWEAR.
NEVER SPEAK TO THEM WITHOUT ME. NEVER!
CHARLIE, PLEASE. I CAN'T DO THIS ANYMORE. I WANT OUT.
OUT?
WE ARE ONE WEEK FROM THE PRIMARIES. ONE WEEK FROM MY NOMINATION.
LISTEN CAREFULLY, YOU STUPID SLUT -- YOU ARE MY HAPPY AND FAITHFUL WIFE. YOU WILL GODDAMN PULL YOURSELF TOGETHER AND REJOIN THE PARTY.
THERE'S THREE MILLION IN BACKERS OUT THERE. AND YOU WILL STICK YOUR TITS IN THEIR FACES TILL THAT MONEY IS MINE.
UNDERSTAND... DEAR?

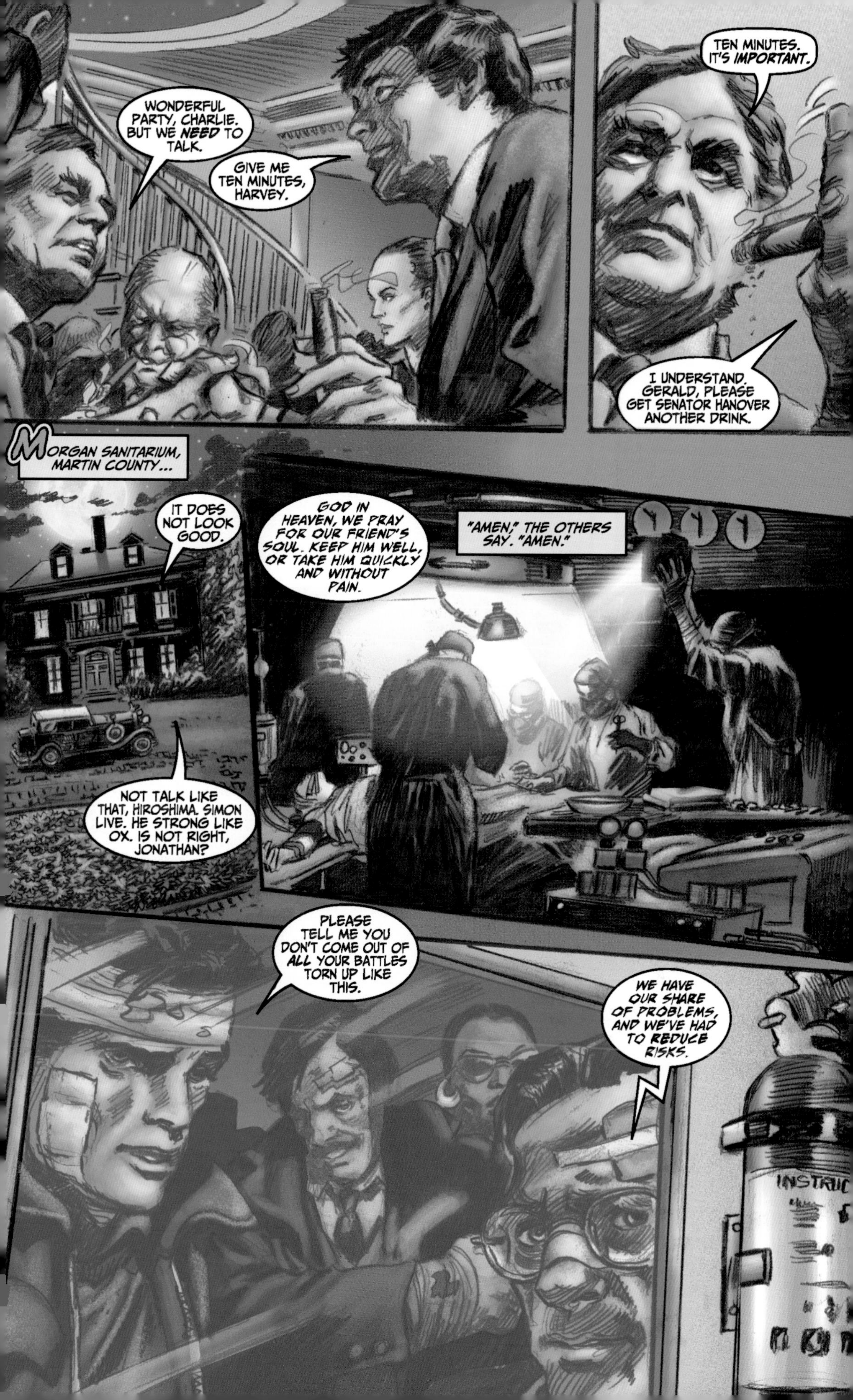
WONDERFUL PARTY, CHARLIE. BUT WE NEED TO TALK.
GIVE ME TEN MINUTES, HARVEY.
TEN MINUTES. IT'S IMPORTANT.
I UNDERSTAND. GERALD, PLEASE GET SENATOR HANOVER ANOTHER DRINK.
MORGAN SANITARIUM, MARTIN COUNTY...
IT DOES NOT LOOK GOOD.
NOT TALK LIKE THAT, HIROSHIMA. SIMON LIVE. HE STRONG LIKE OX. IS NOT RIGHT, JONATHAN?
GOD IN HEAVEN, WE PRAY FOR OUR FRIEND'S SOUL. KEEP HIM WELL, OR TAKE HIM QUICKLY AND WITHOUT PAIN.
"AMEN," THE OTHERS SAY. "AMEN."
PLEASE TELL ME YOU DON'T COME OUT OF ALL YOUR BATTLES TORN UP LIKE THIS.
WE HAVE OUR SHARE OF PROBLEMS, AND WE'VE HAD TO REDUCE RISKS.
INSTRUC

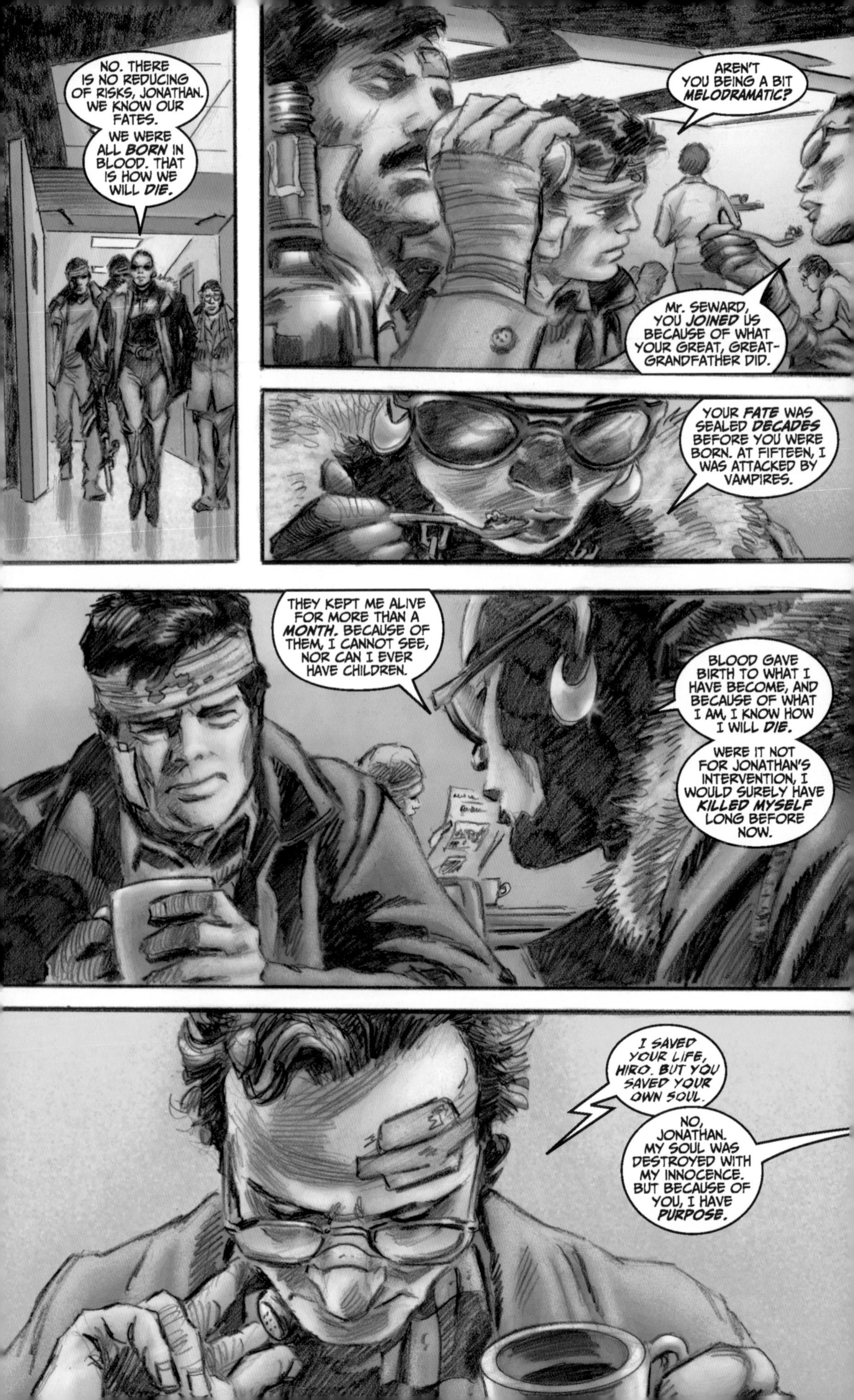
NO. THERE IS NO REDUCING OF RISKS, JONATHAN. WE KNOW OUR FATES.
WE WERE ALL BORN IN BLOOD. THAT IS HOW WE WILL DIE.
AREN'T YOU BEING A BIT MELODRAMATIC?
Mr. SEWARD, YOU JOINED US BECAUSE OF WHAT YOUR GREAT, GREAT-GRANDFATHER DID.
YOUR FATE WAS SEALED DECADES BEFORE YOU WERE BORN. AT FIFTEEN, I WAS ATTACKED BY VAMPIRES.
THEY KEPT ME ALIVE FOR MORE THAN A MONTH. BECAUSE OF THEM, I CANNOT SEE, NOR CAN I EVER HAVE CHILDREN.
BLOOD GAVE BIRTH TO WHAT I HAVE BECOME, AND BECAUSE OF WHAT I AM, I KNOW HOW I WILL DIE.
WERE IT NOT FOR JONATHAN'S INTERVENTION, I WOULD SURELY HAVE KILLED MYSELF LONG BEFORE NOW.
I SAVED YOUR LIFE, HIRO. BUT YOU SAVED YOUR OWN SOUL.
NO, JONATHAN. MY SOUL WAS DESTROYED WITH MY INNOCENCE. BUT BECAUSE OF YOU, I HAVE PURPOSE.

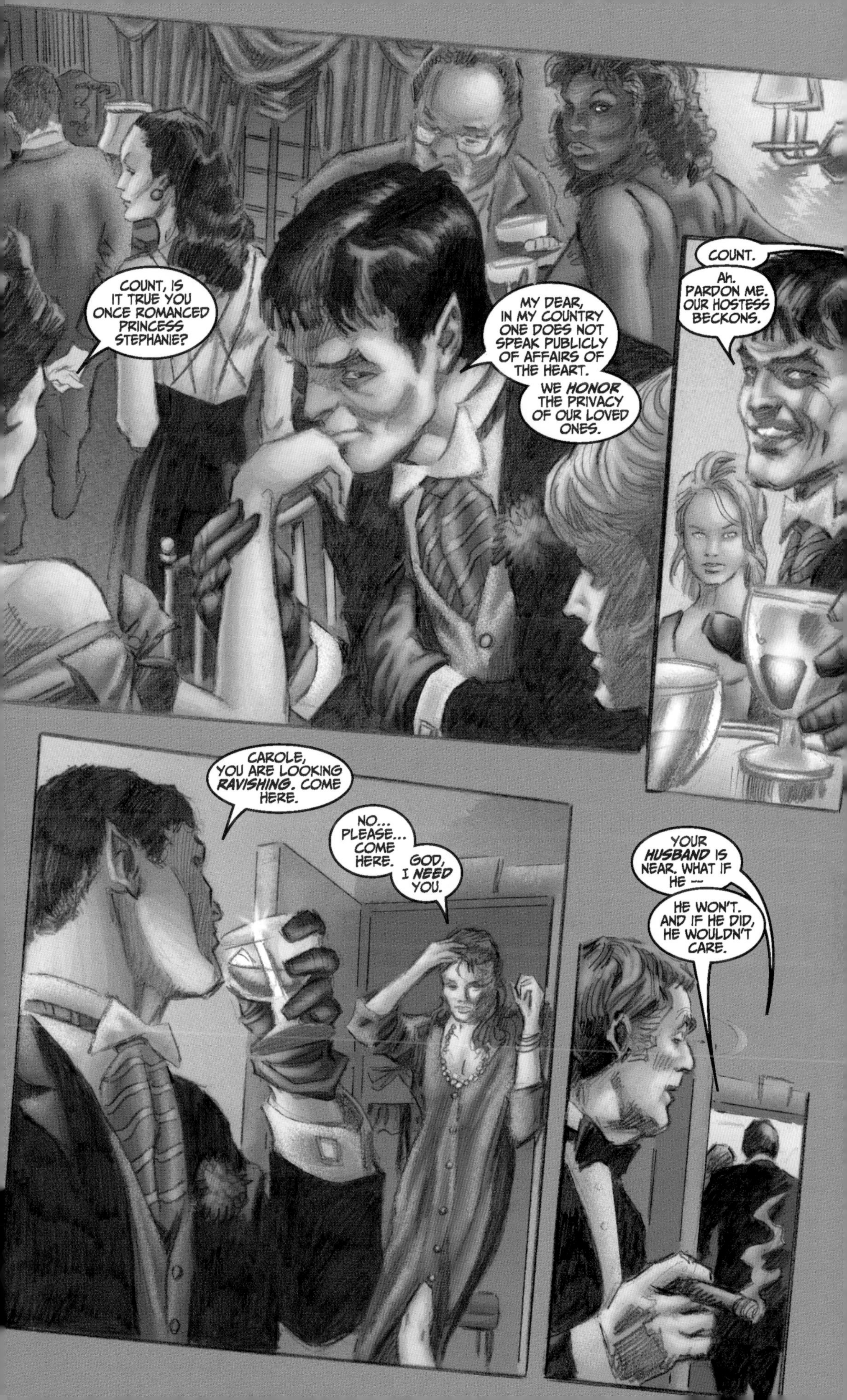

COUNT, IS IT TRUE YOU ONCE ROMANCED PRINCESS STEPHANIE?
MY DEAR, IN MY COUNTRY ONE DOES NOT SPEAK PUBLICLY OF AFFAIRS OF THE HEART.
WE HONOR THE PRIVACY OF OUR LOVED ONES.
COUNT.
Ah. PARDON ME. OUR HOSTESS BECKONS.
CAROLE, YOU ARE LOOKING RAVISHING. COME HERE.
NO... PLEASE... COME HERE.
GOD, I NEED YOU.
YOUR HUSBAND IS NEAR. WHAT IF HE --
HE WON'T. AND IF HE DID, HE WOULDN'T CARE.

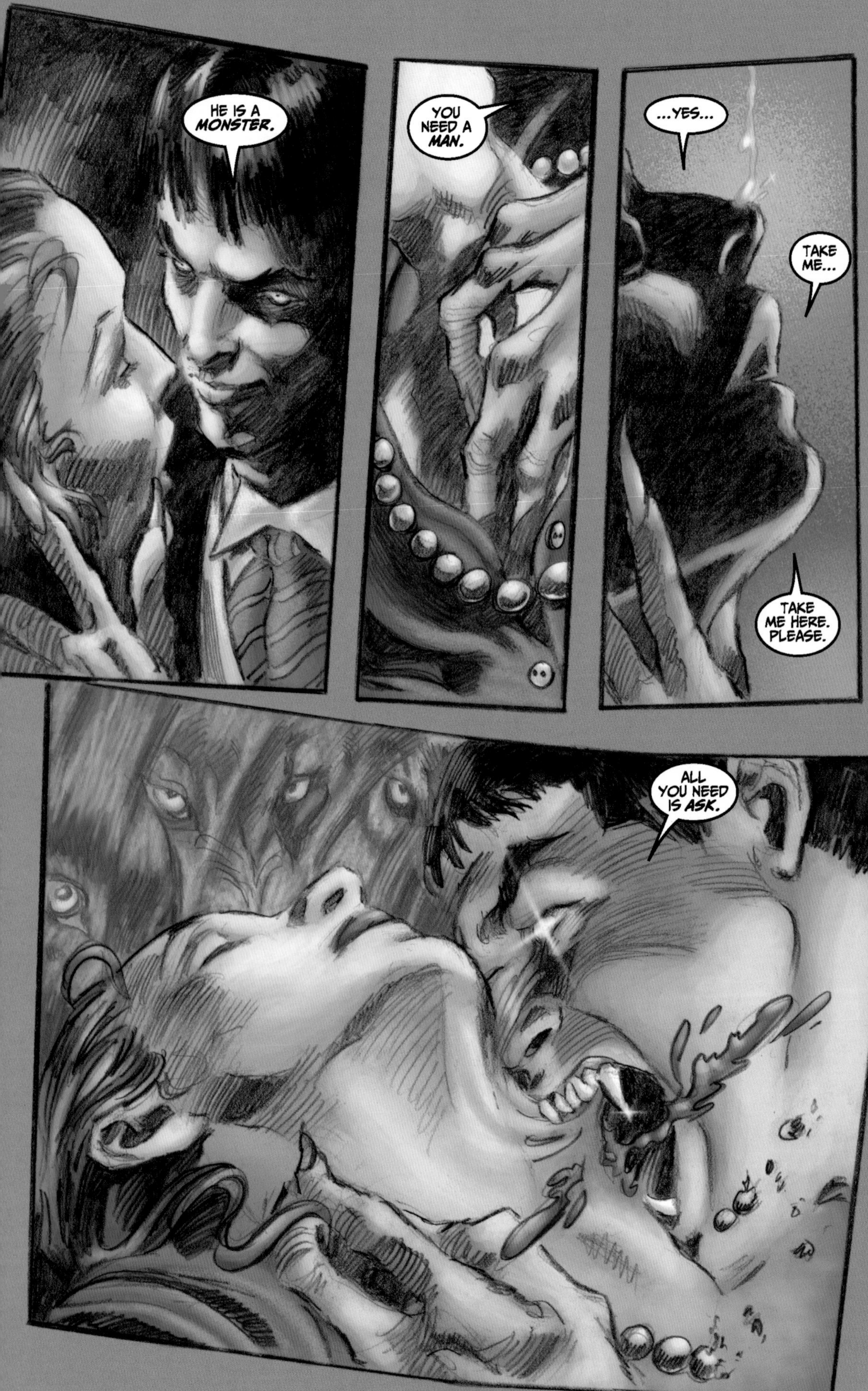
HE IS A MONSTER.
YOU NEED A MAN.
...YES...
TAKE ME...
TAKE ME HERE. PLEASE.
ALL YOU NEED IS ASK.

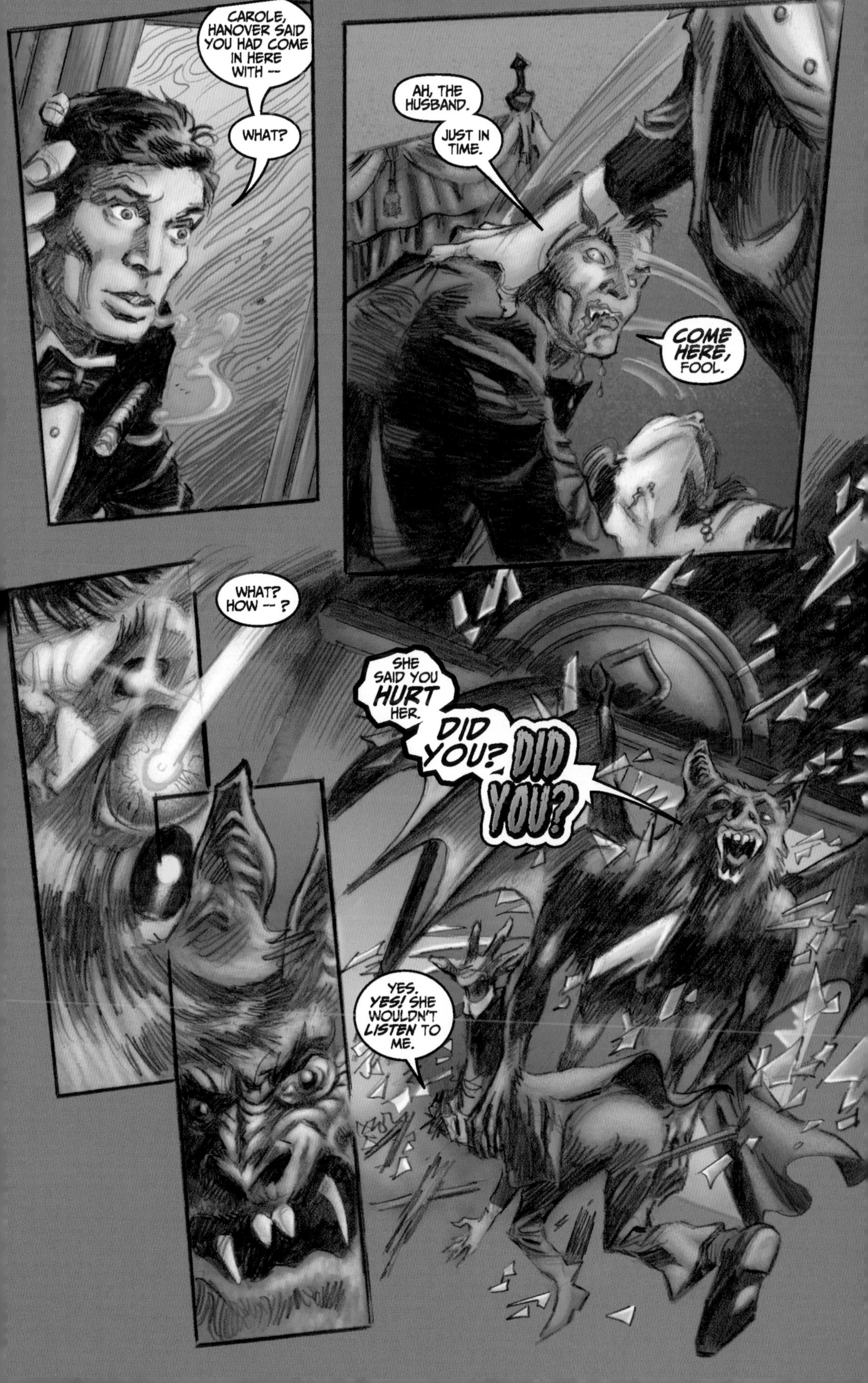
CAROLE, HANOVER SAID YOU HAD COME IN HERE WITH --
WHAT?
AH, THE HUSBAND.
JUST IN TIME.
COME HERE, FOOL.
WHAT? HOW -- ?
SHE SAID YOU HURT HER.
DID YOU?
DID YOU?
YES. YES! SHE WOULDN'T LISTEN TO ME.

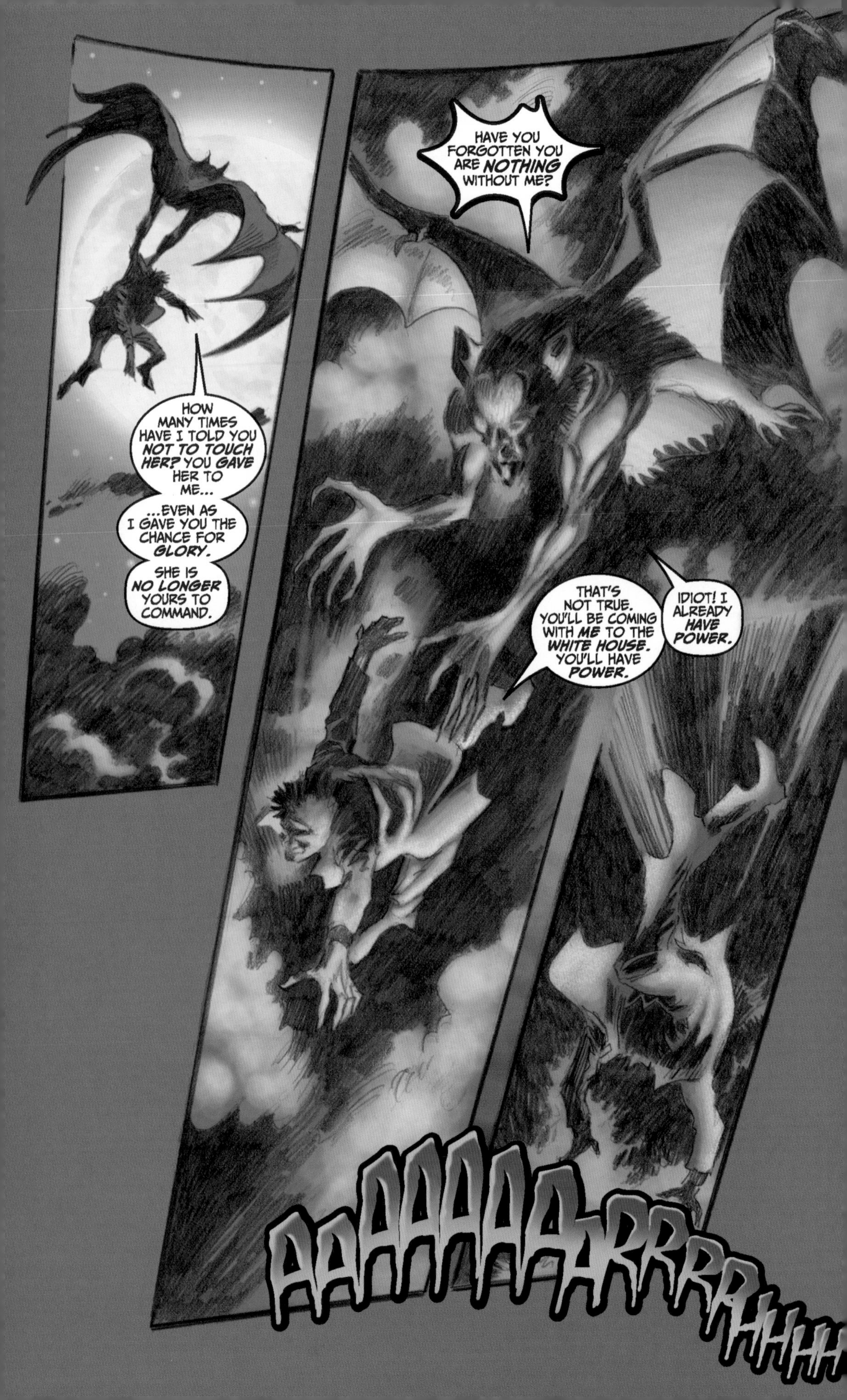
HOW MANY TIMES HAVE I TOLD YOU NOT TO TOUCH HER? YOU GAVE HER TO ME...
...EVEN AS I GAVE YOU THE CHANCE FOR GLORY.
SHE IS NO LONGER YOURS TO COMMAND.
HAVE YOU FORGOTTEN YOU ARE NOTHING WITHOUT ME?
THAT'S NOT TRUE. YOU'LL BE COMING WITH ME TO THE WHITE HOUSE. YOU'LL HAVE POWER.
IDIOT! I ALREADY HAVE POWER.
AAAAAAARRRRRHHHH

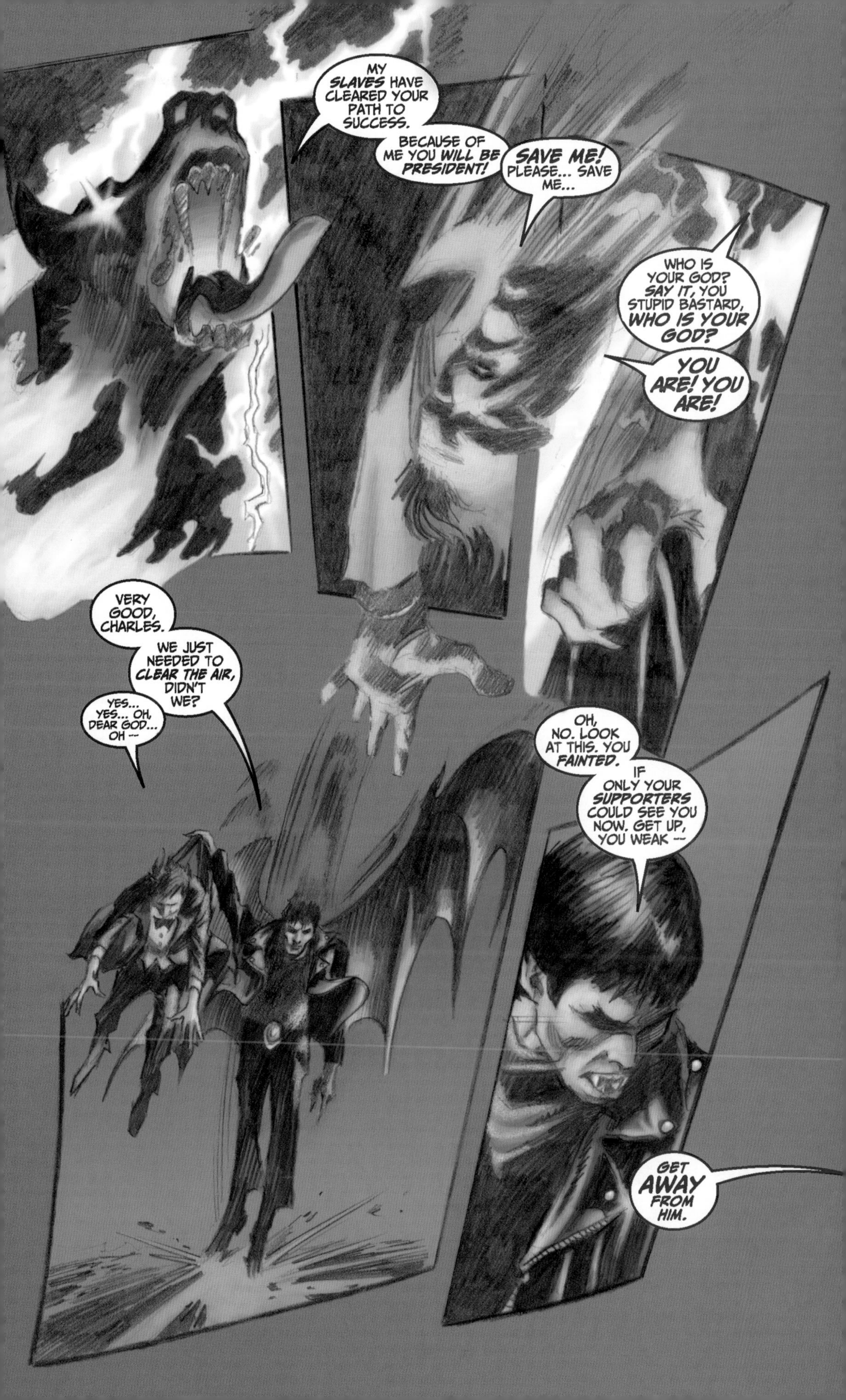
MY SLAVES HAVE CLEARED YOUR PATH TO SUCCESS.
BECAUSE OF ME YOU WILL BE PRESIDENT!
SAVE ME! PLEASE... SAVE ME...
WHO IS YOUR GOD? SAY IT, YOU STUPID BASTARD, WHO IS YOUR GOD?
YOU ARE! YOU ARE!
VERY GOOD, CHARLES.
WE JUST NEEDED TO CLEAR THE AIR, DIDN'T WE?
YES... YES... OH, DEAR GOD... OH --
OH, NO. LOOK AT THIS. YOU FAINTED.
IF ONLY YOUR SUPPORTERS COULD SEE YOU NOW. GET UP, YOU WEAK --
GET AWAY FROM HIM.

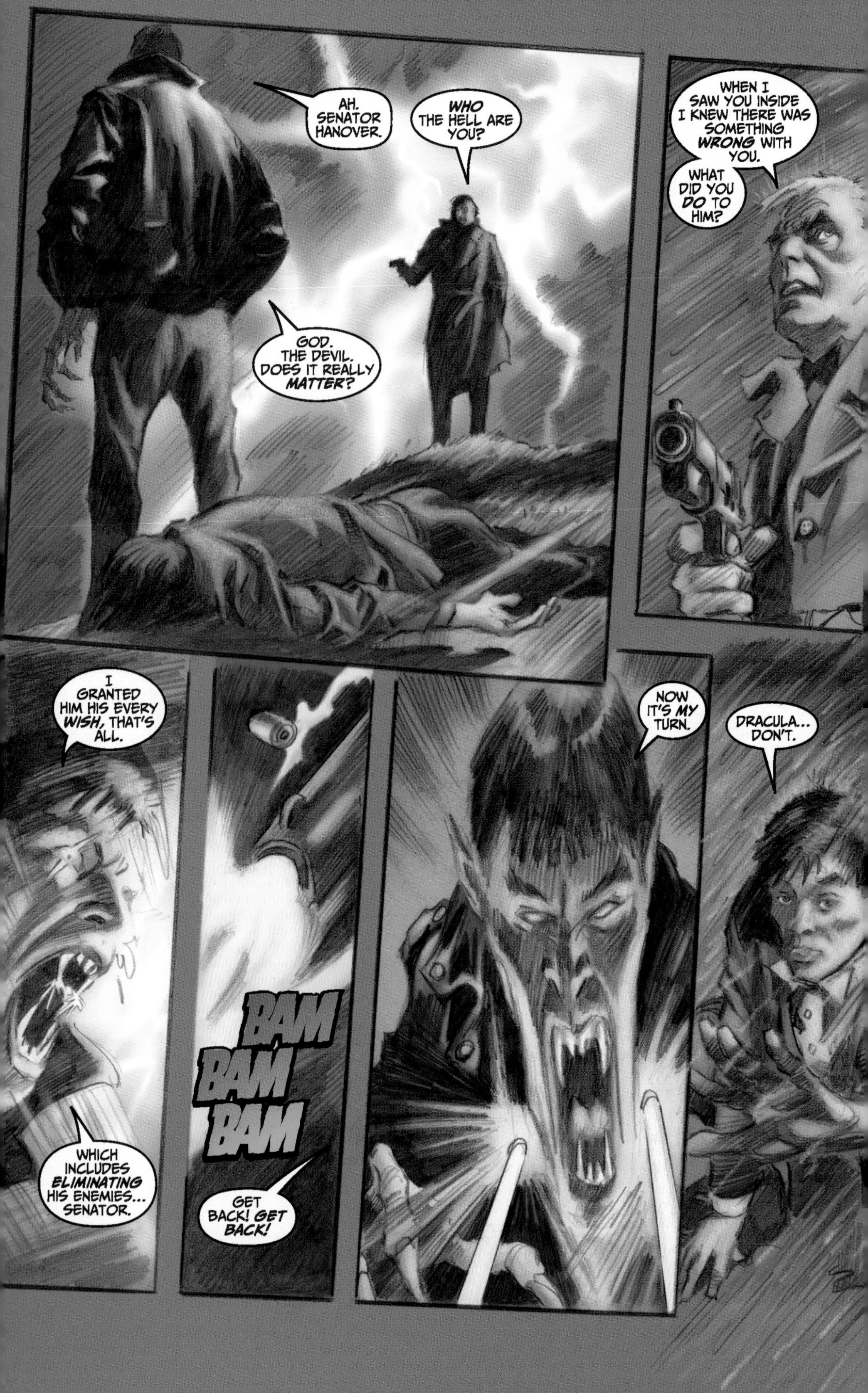
AH. SENATOR HANOVER.
WHO THE HELL ARE YOU?
GOD. THE DEVIL. DOES IT REALLY MATTER?
WHEN I SAW YOU INSIDE I KNEW THERE WAS SOMETHING WRONG WITH YOU.
WHAT DID YOU DO TO HIM?
I GRANTED HIM HIS EVERY WISH, THAT'S ALL.
WHICH INCLUDES ELIMINATING HIS ENEMIES... SENATOR.
BAM
BAM
BAM
GET BACK! GET BACK!
NOW IT'S MY TURN.
DRACULA... DON'T.

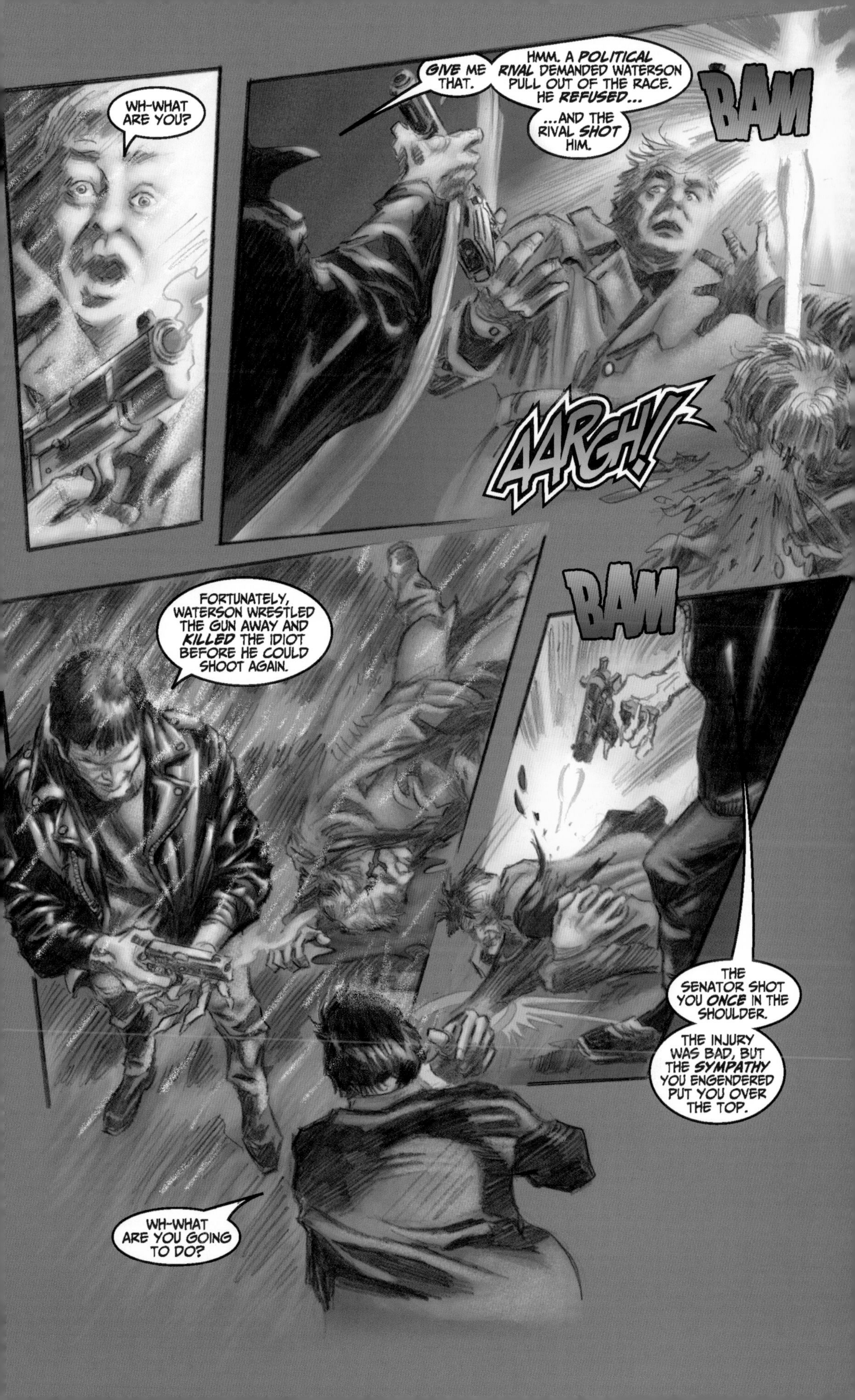
WH-WHAT ARE YOU?
GIVE ME THAT.
HMM. A POLITICAL RIVAL DEMANDED WATERSON PULL OUT OF THE RACE. HE REFUSED...
...AND THE RIVAL SHOT HIM.
BAM
AARGH!!
BAM
FORTUNATELY, WATERSON WRESTLED THE GUN AWAY AND KILLED THE IDIOT BEFORE HE COULD SHOOT AGAIN.
THE SENATOR SHOT YOU ONCE IN THE SHOULDER.
THE INJURY WAS BAD, BUT THE SYMPATHY YOU ENGENDERED PUT YOU OVER THE TOP.
WH-WHAT ARE YOU GOING TO DO?

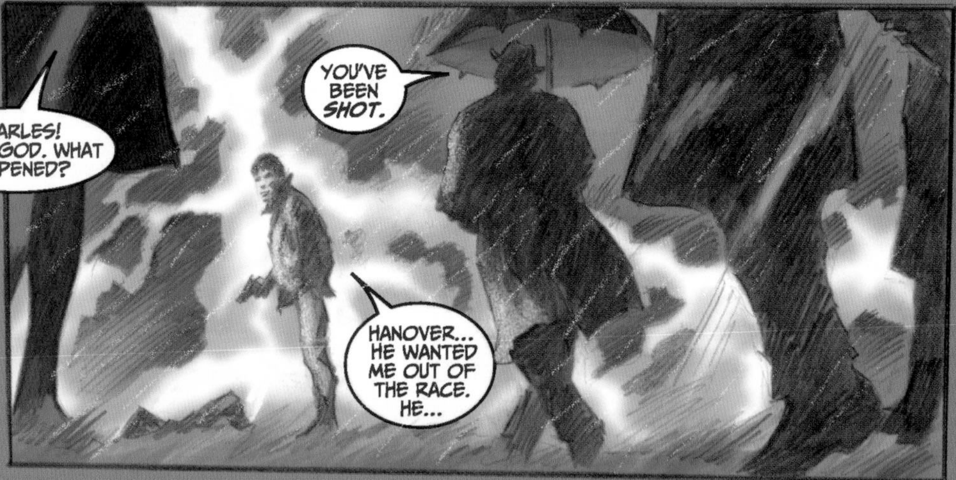
CHARLES! OH MY GOD. WHAT HAPPENED?
YOU'VE BEEN SHOT.
HANOVER... HE WANTED ME OUT OF THE RACE. HE...

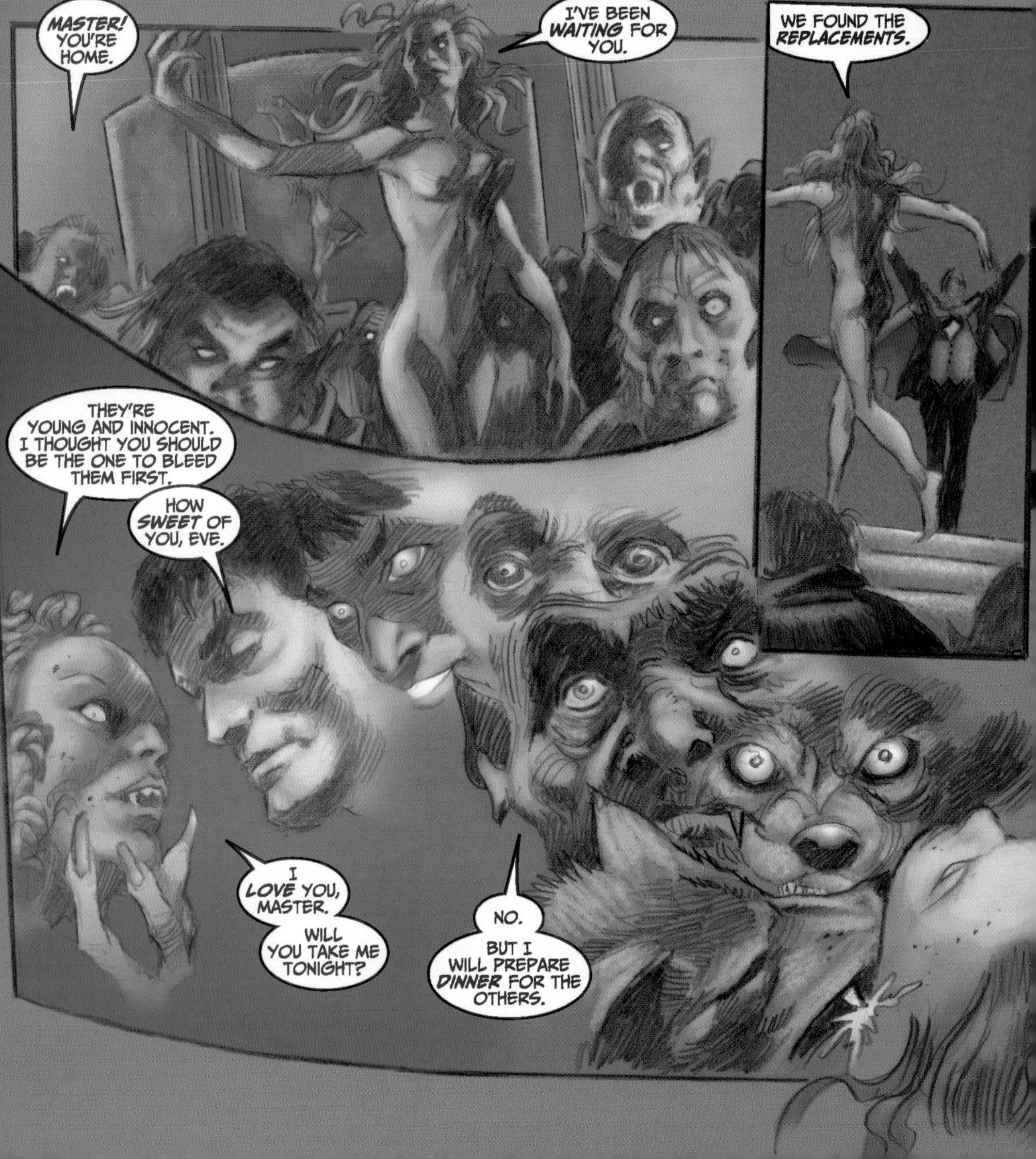
MASTER! YOU'RE HOME.
I'VE BEEN WAITING FOR YOU.
WE FOUND THE REPLACEMENTS.
THEY'RE YOUNG AND INNOCENT. I THOUGHT YOU SHOULD BE THE ONE TO BLEED THEM FIRST.
HOW SWEET OF YOU, EVE.
I LOVE YOU, MASTER.
WILL YOU TAKE ME TONIGHT?
NO.
BUT I WILL PREPARE DINNER FOR THE OTHERS.

Chapter III

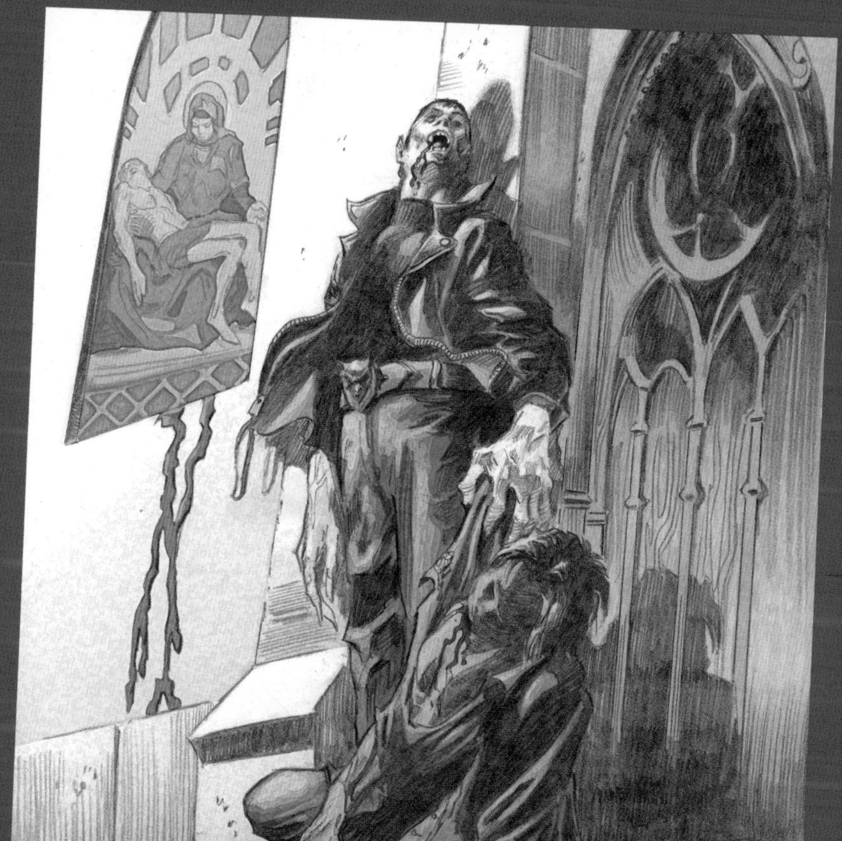
Gene Colan

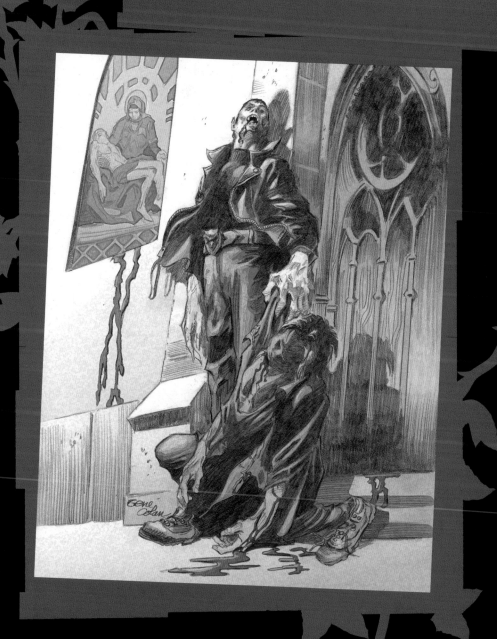

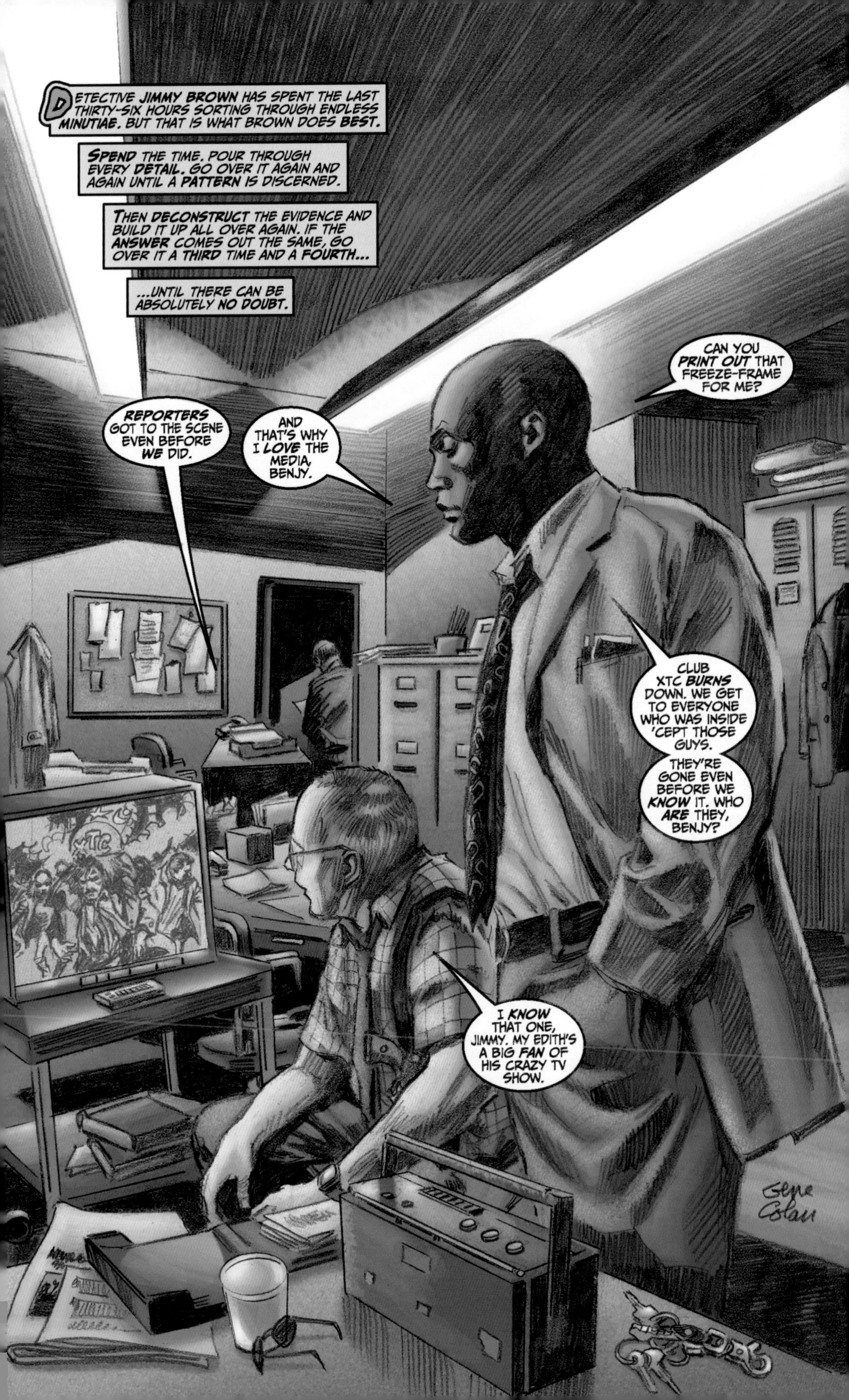
DETECTIVE JIMMY BROWN HAS SPENT THE LAST THIRTY-SIX HOURS SORTING THROUGH ENDLESS MINUTIAE. BUT THAT IS WHAT BROWN DOES BEST.
SPEND THE TIME. POUR THROUGH EVERY DETAIL. GO OVER IT AGAIN AND AGAIN UNTIL A PATTERN IS DISCERNED.
THEN DECONSTRUCT THE EVIDENCE AND BUILD IT UP ALL OVER AGAIN. IF THE ANSWER COMES OUT THE SAME, GO OVER IT A THIRD TIME AND A FOURTH...
...UNTIL THERE CAN BE ABSOLUTELY NO DOUBT.
REPORTERS GOT TO THE SCENE EVEN BEFORE WE DID.
AND THAT'S WHY I LOVE THE MEDIA, BENJY.
CAN YOU PRINT OUT THAT FREEZE-FRAME FOR ME?
CLUB XTC BURNS DOWN. WE GET TO EVERYONE WHO WAS INSIDE 'CEPT THOSE GUYS.
THEY'RE GONE EVEN BEFORE WE KNOW IT. WHO ARE THEY, BENJY?
I KNOW THAT ONE, JIMMY. MY EDITH'S A BIG FAN OF HIS CRAZY TV SHOW.
Gene Colan

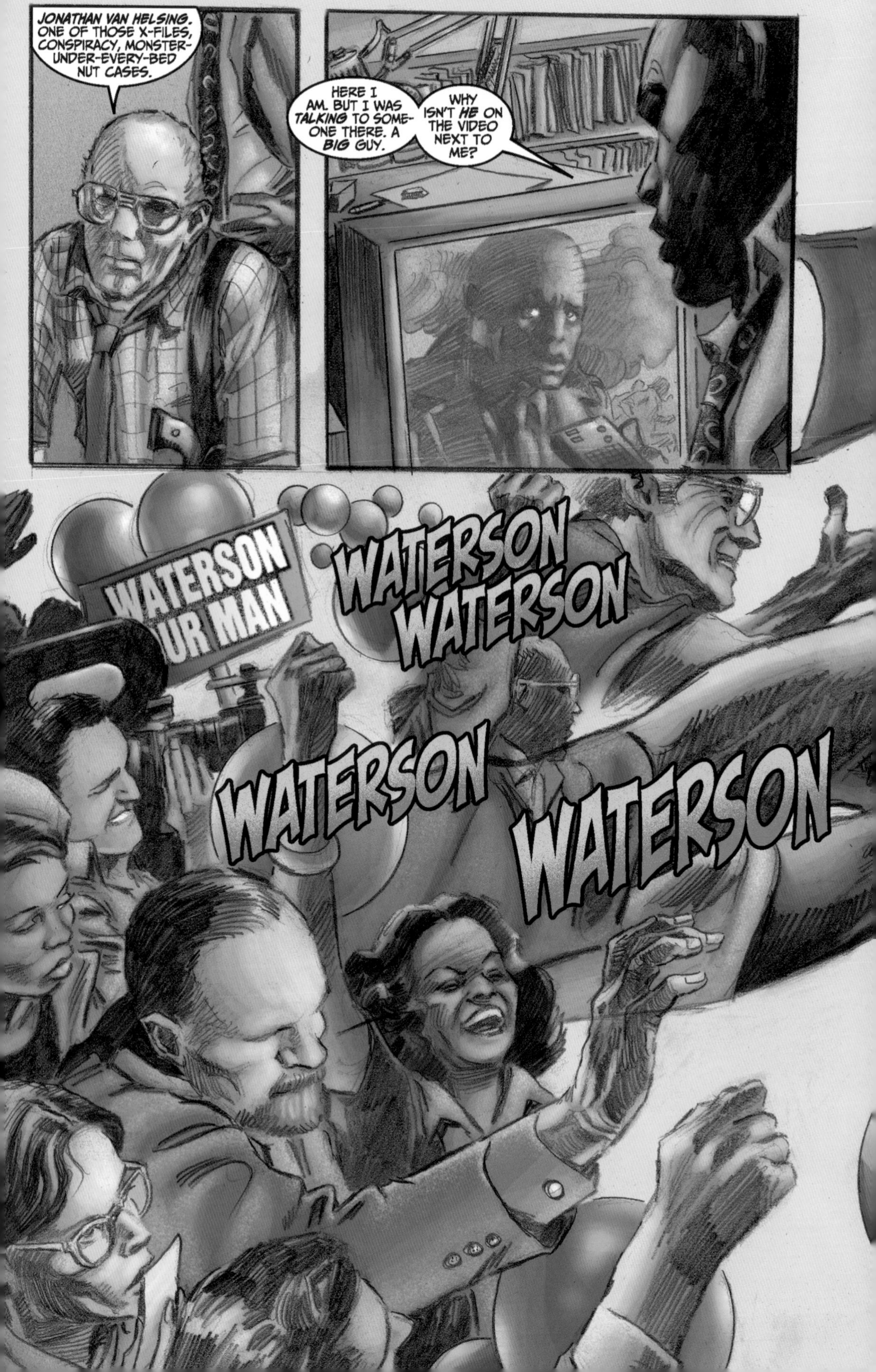
JONATHAN VAN HELSING. ONE OF THOSE X-FILES, CONSPIRACY, MONSTER-UNDER-EVERY-BED NUT CASES.
HERE I AM. BUT I WAS TALKING TO SOME-ONE THERE. A BIG GUY.
WHY ISN'T HE ON THE VIDEO NEXT TO ME?
WATERSON
UR MAN
WATERSON
WATERSON
WATERSON
WATERSON

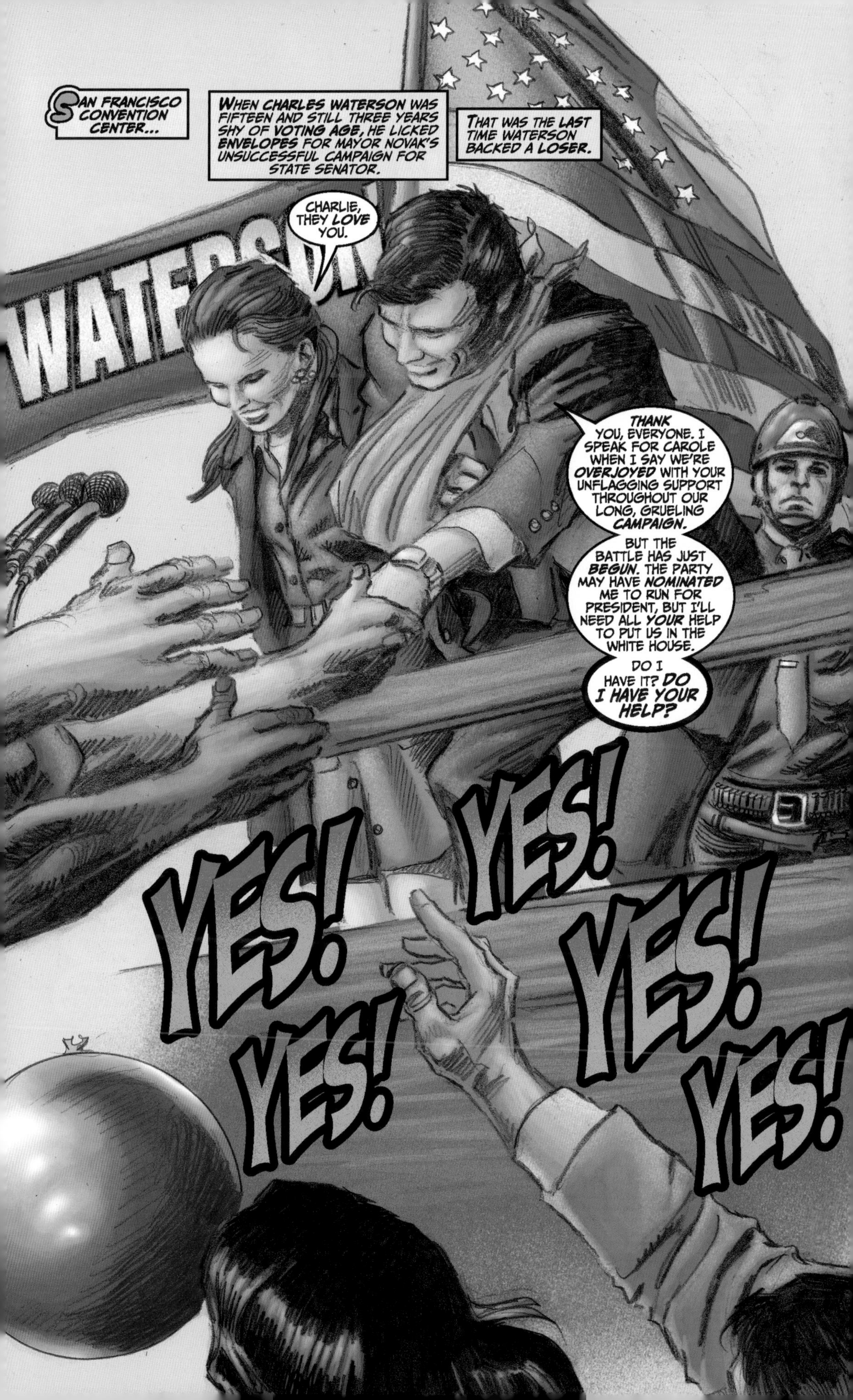
SAN FRANCISCO CONVENTION CENTER...
WHEN CHARLES WATERSON WAS FIFTEEN AND STILL THREE YEARS SHY OF VOTING AGE, HE LICKED ENVELOPES FOR MAYOR NOVAK'S UNSUCCESSFUL CAMPAIGN FOR STATE SENATOR.
THAT WAS THE LAST TIME WATERSON BACKED A LOSER.
CHARLIE, THEY LOVE YOU.
THANK YOU, EVERYONE. I SPEAK FOR CAROLE WHEN I SAY WE'RE OVERJOYED WITH YOUR UNFLAGGING SUPPORT THROUGHOUT OUR LONG, GRUELING CAMPAIGN.
BUT THE BATTLE HAS JUST BEGUN. THE PARTY MAY HAVE NOMINATED ME TO RUN FOR PRESIDENT, BUT I'LL NEED ALL YOUR HELP TO PUT US IN THE WHITE HOUSE.
DO I HAVE IT? DO I HAVE YOUR HELP?
YES! YES!
YES! YES!
YES! YES!

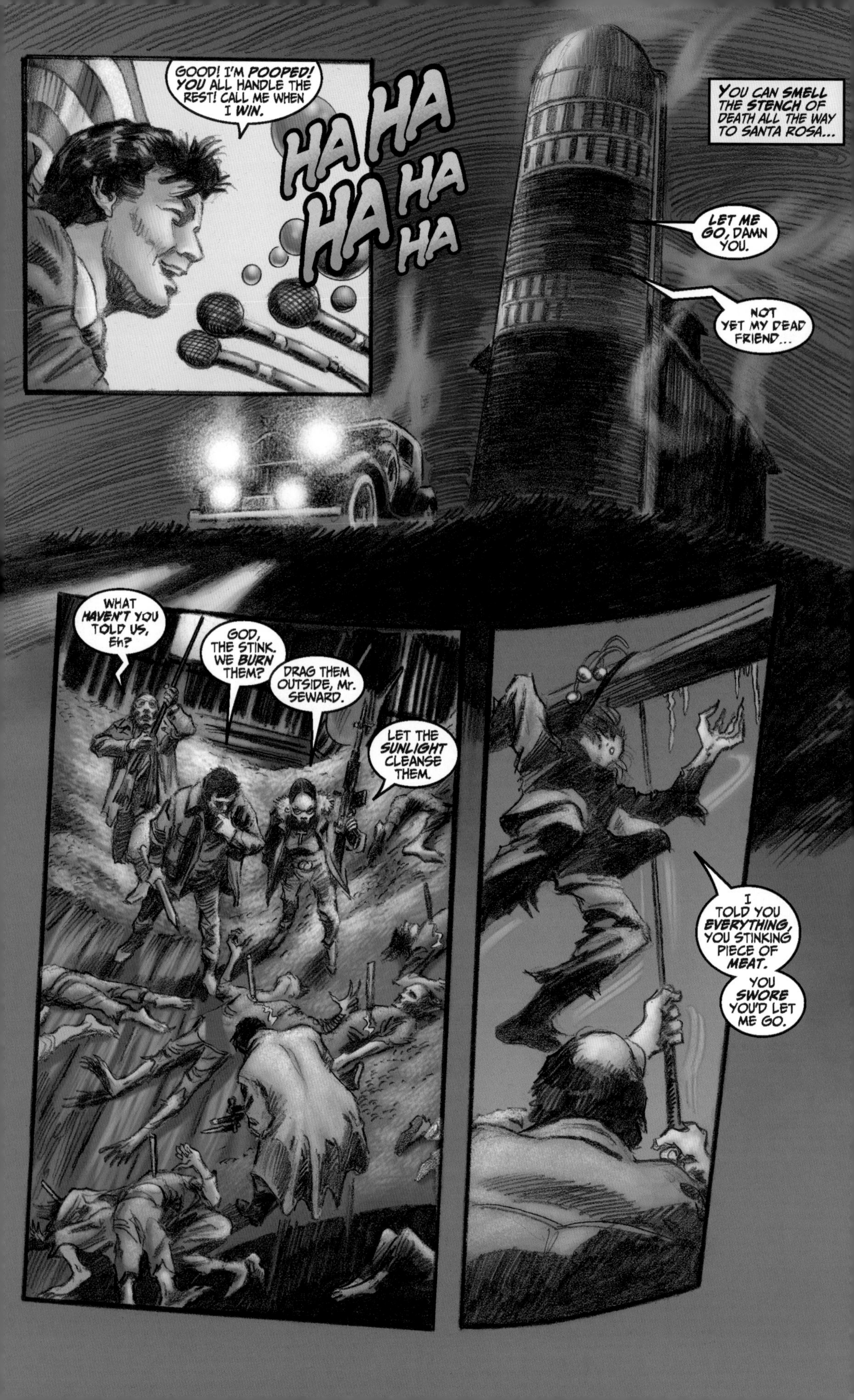
GOOD! I'M POOPED! YOU ALL HANDLE THE REST! CALL ME WHEN I WIN.
HA HA HA HA HA
YOU CAN SMELL THE STENCH OF DEATH ALL THE WAY TO SANTA ROSA...
LET ME GO, DAMN YOU.
NOT YET MY DEAD FRIEND...
WHAT HAVEN'T YOU TOLD US, Eh?
GOD, THE STINK. WE BURN THEM?
DRAG THEM OUTSIDE, Mr. SEWARD.
LET THE SUNLIGHT CLEANSE THEM.
I TOLD YOU EVERYTHING, YOU STINKING PIECE OF MEAT.
YOU SWORE YOU'D LET ME GO.

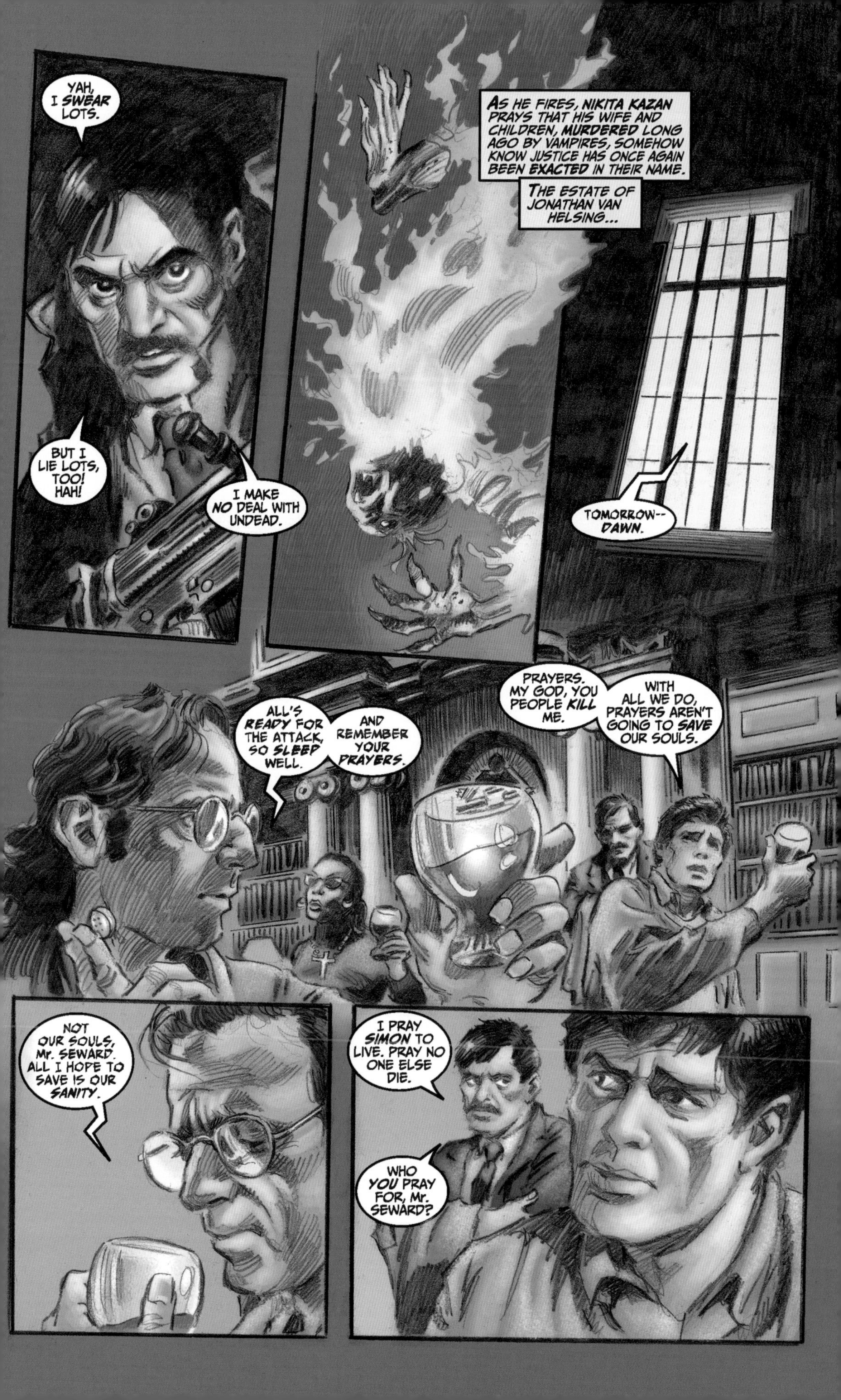
YAH, I SWEAR LOTS.
BUT I LIE LOTS, TOO! HAH!
I MAKE NO DEAL WITH UNDEAD.
AS HE FIRES, NIKITA KAZAN PRAYS THAT HIS WIFE AND CHILDREN, MURDERED LONG AGO BY VAMPIRES, SOMEHOW KNOW JUSTICE HAS ONCE AGAIN BEEN EXACTED IN THEIR NAME.
THE ESTATE OF JONATHAN VAN HELSING...
TOMORROW-- DAWN.
ALL'S READY FOR THE ATTACK, SO SLEEP WELL.
AND REMEMBER YOUR PRAYERS.
PRAYERS. MY GOD, YOU PEOPLE KILL ME.
WITH ALL WE DO, PRAYERS AREN'T GOING TO SAVE OUR SOULS.
NOT OUR SOULS, Mr. SEWARD. ALL I HOPE TO SAVE IS OUR SANITY.
I PRAY SIMON TO LIVE. PRAY NO ONE ELSE DIE.
WHO YOU PRAY FOR, Mr. SEWARD?

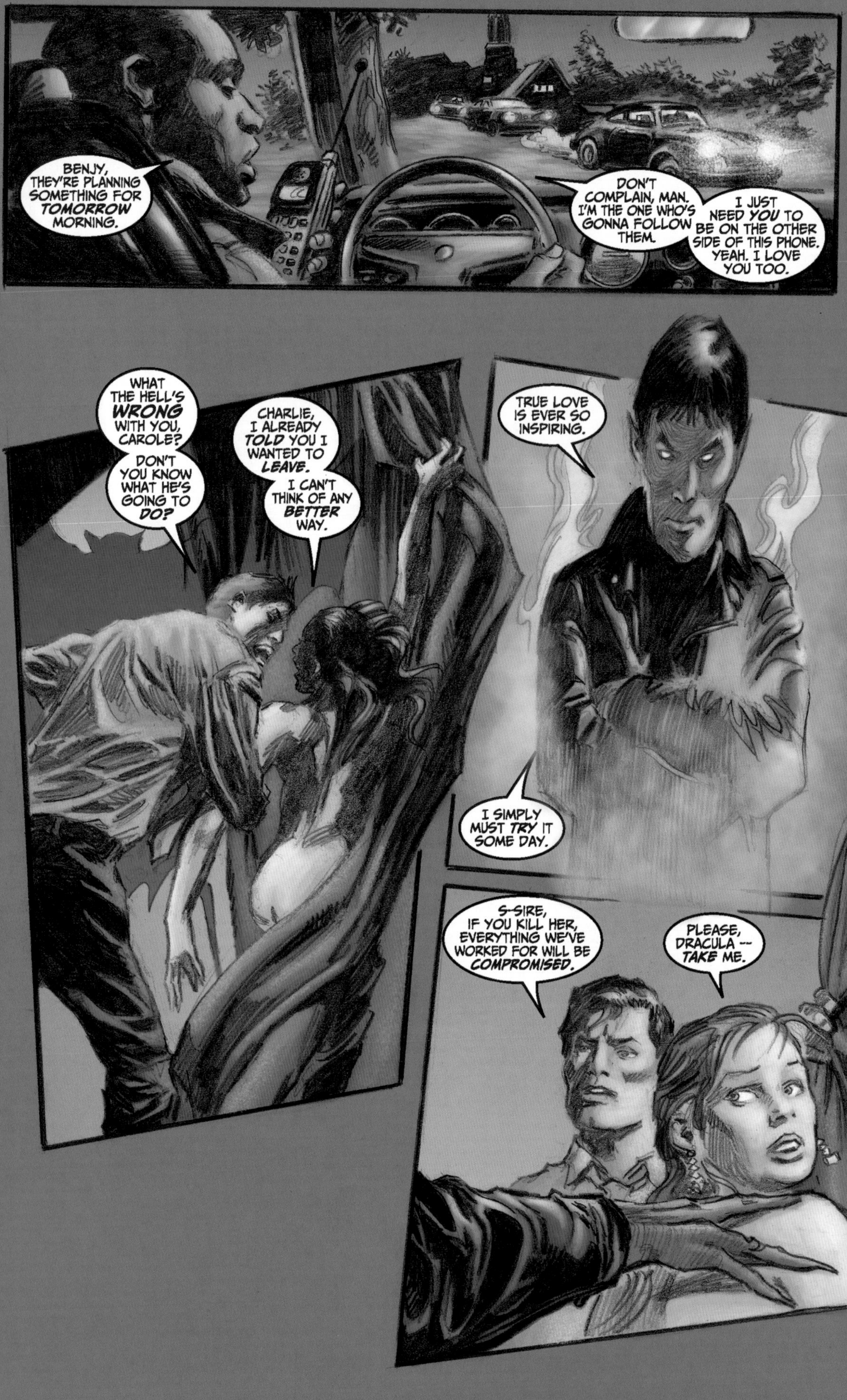
BENJY, THEY'RE PLANNING SOMETHING FOR TOMORROW MORNING.
DON'T COMPLAIN, MAN. I'M THE ONE WHO'S GONNA FOLLOW THEM.
I JUST NEED YOU TO BE ON THE OTHER SIDE OF THIS PHONE. YEAH. I LOVE YOU TOO.
WHAT THE HELL'S WRONG WITH YOU, CAROLE?
DON'T YOU KNOW WHAT HE'S GOING TO DO?
CHARLIE, I ALREADY TOLD YOU I WANTED TO LEAVE.
I CAN'T THINK OF ANY BETTER WAY.
TRUE LOVE IS EVER SO INSPIRING.
I SIMPLY MUST TRY IT SOME DAY.
S-SIRE, IF YOU KILL HER, EVERYTHING WE'VE WORKED FOR WILL BE COMPROMISED.
PLEASE, DRACULA -- TAKE ME.

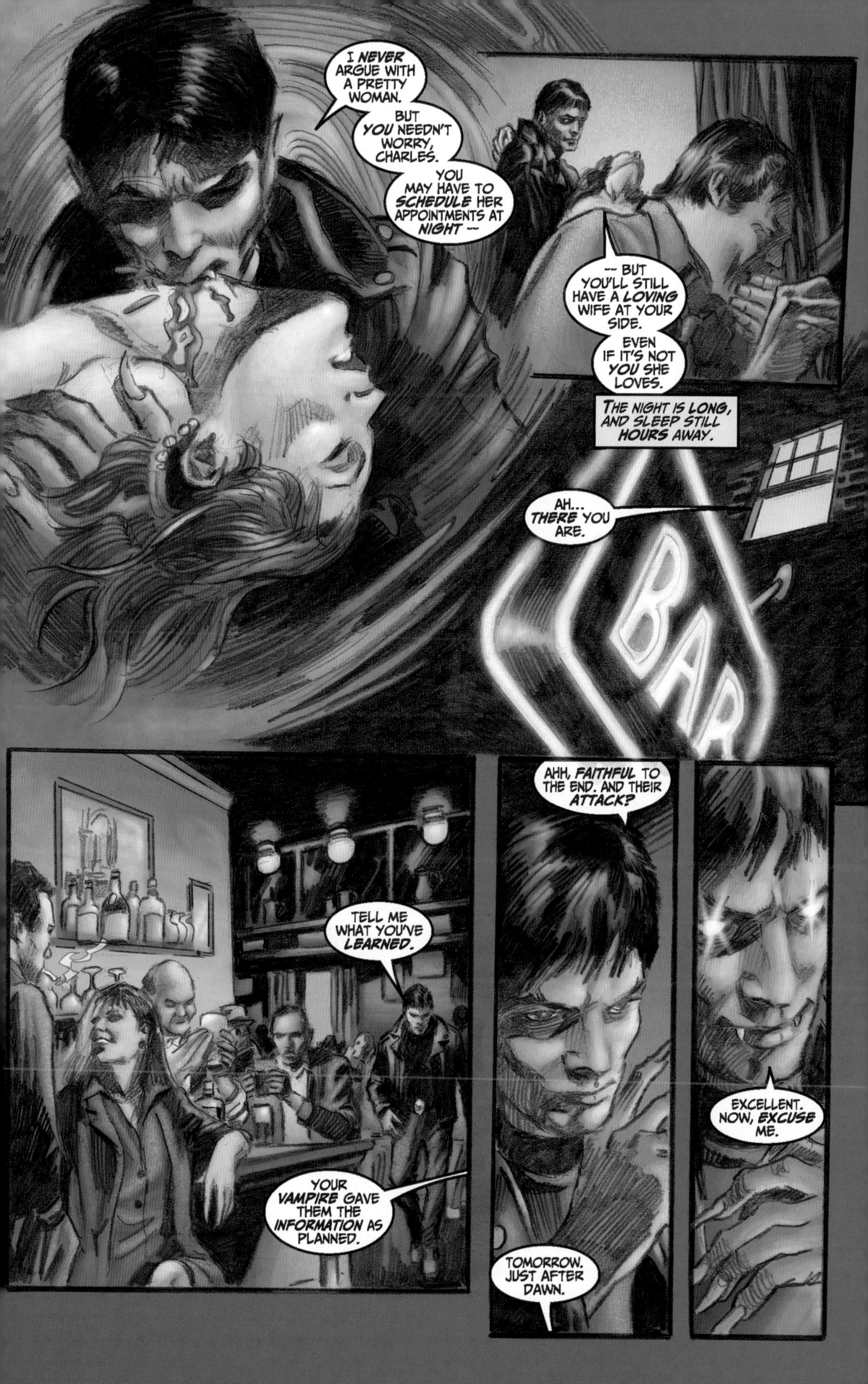
I NEVER ARGUE WITH A PRETTY WOMAN.
BUT YOU NEEDN'T WORRY, CHARLES.
YOU MAY HAVE TO SCHEDULE HER APPOINTMENTS AT NIGHT --
-- BUT YOU'LL STILL HAVE A LOVING WIFE AT YOUR SIDE.
EVEN IF IT'S NOT YOU SHE LOVES.
THE NIGHT IS LONG, AND SLEEP STILL HOURS AWAY.
AH... THERE YOU ARE.
BAR
TELL ME WHAT YOU'VE LEARNED.
YOUR VAMPIRE GAVE THEM THE INFORMATION AS PLANNED.
AHH, FAITHFUL TO THE END. AND THEIR ATTACK?
TOMORROW. JUST AFTER DAWN.
EXCELLENT. NOW, EXCUSE ME.

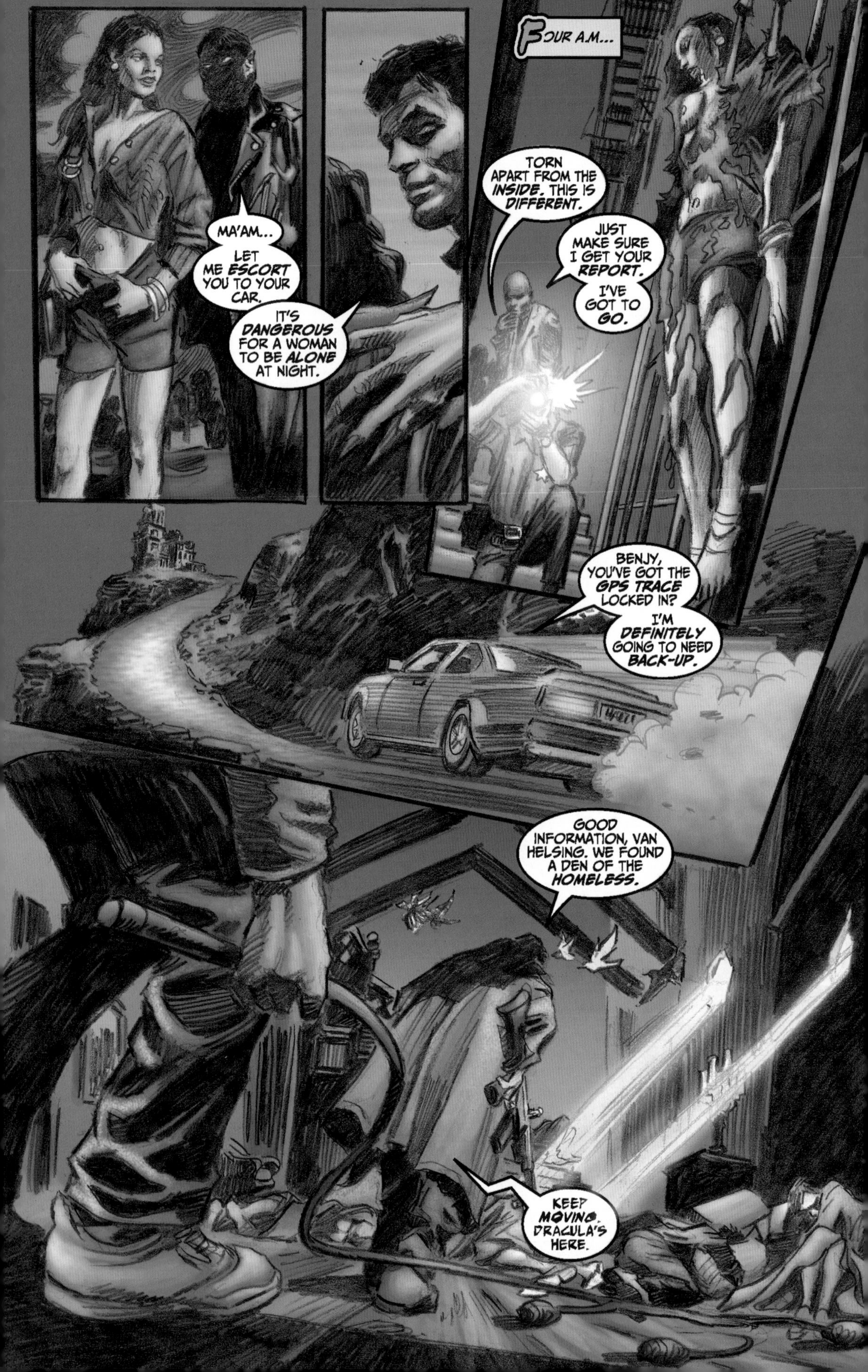
MA'AM...
LET ME ESCORT YOU TO YOUR CAR.
IT'S DANGEROUS FOR A WOMAN TO BE ALONE AT NIGHT.
FOUR A.M...
TORN APART FROM THE INSIDE. THIS IS DIFFERENT.
JUST MAKE SURE I GET YOUR REPORT.
I'VE GOT TO GO.
BENJY, YOU'VE GOT THE GPS TRACE LOCKED IN?
I'M DEFINITELY GOING TO NEED BACK-UP.
GOOD INFORMATION, VAN HELSING. WE FOUND A DEN OF THE HOMELESS.
KEEP MOVING. DRACULA'S HERE.

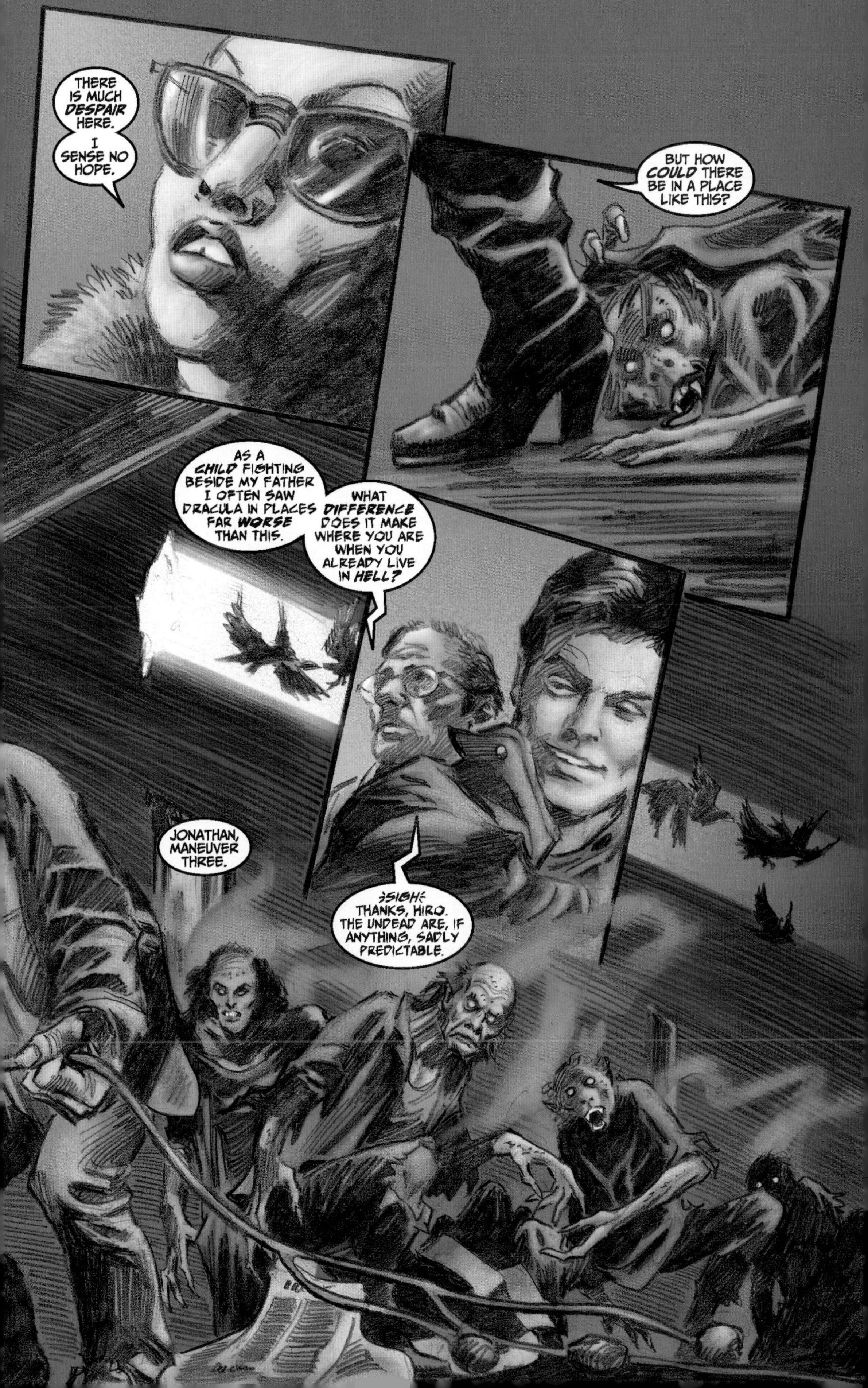
THERE IS MUCH DESPAIR HERE.
I SENSE NO HOPE.
BUT HOW COULD THERE BE IN A PLACE LIKE THIS?
AS A CHILD FIGHTING BESIDE MY FATHER I OFTEN SAW DRACULA IN PLACES FAR WORSE THAN THIS.
WHAT DIFFERENCE DOES IT MAKE WHERE YOU ARE WHEN YOU ALREADY LIVE IN HELL?
JONATHAN, MANEUVER THREE.
SIGH
THANKS, HIRO. THE UNDEAD ARE, IF ANYTHING, SADLY PREDICTABLE.

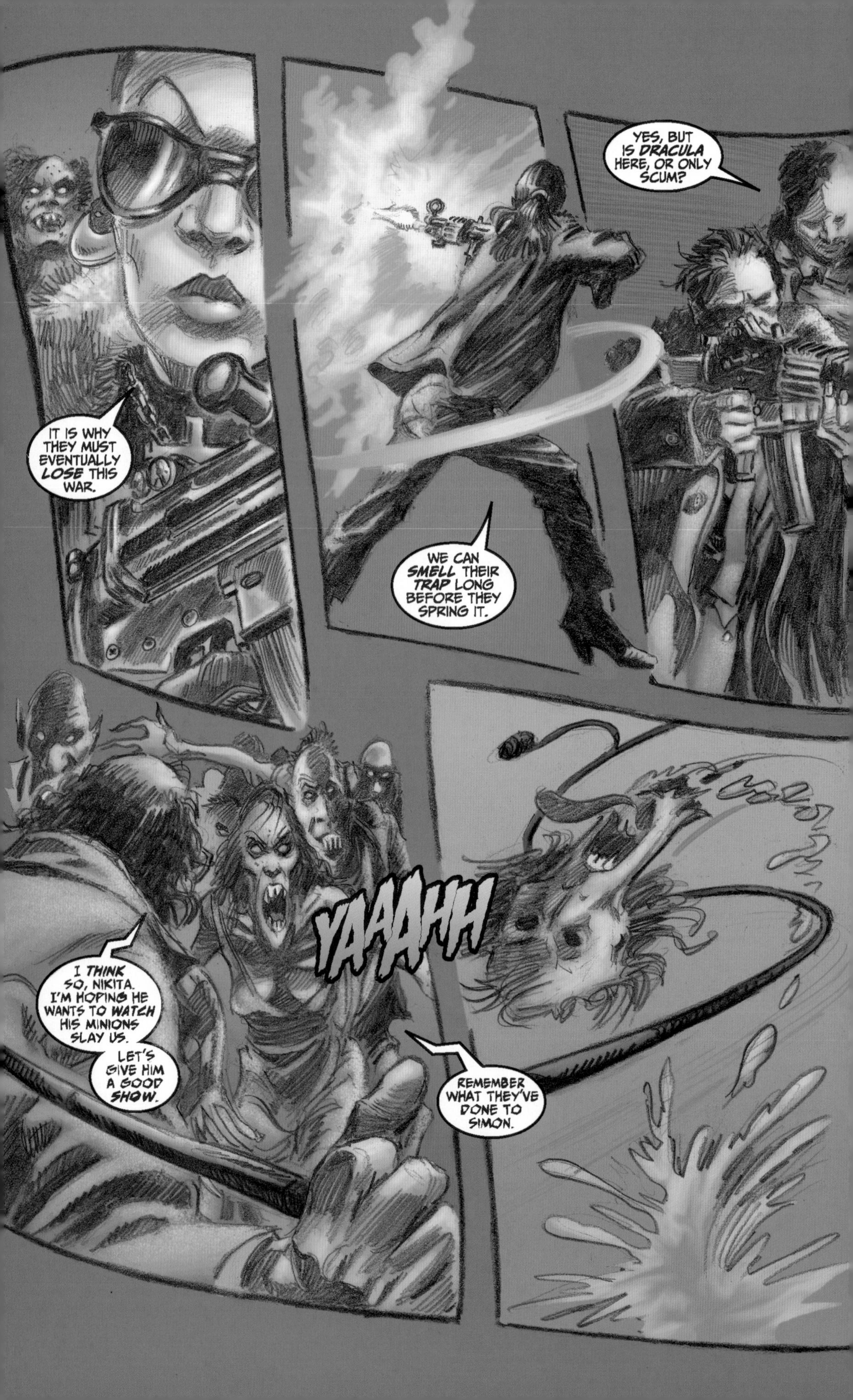

IT IS WHY THEY MUST EVENTUALLY *LOSE* THIS WAR.
WE CAN *SMELL* THEIR *TRAP* LONG BEFORE THEY SPRING IT.
YES, BUT IS *DRACULA* HERE, OR ONLY SCUM?
I *THINK* SO, NIKITA. I'M HOPING HE WANTS TO *WATCH* HIS MINIONS SLAY US.
LET'S GIVE HIM A GOOD *SHOW*.
YAAAHH
REMEMBER WHAT THEY'VE DONE TO SIMON.

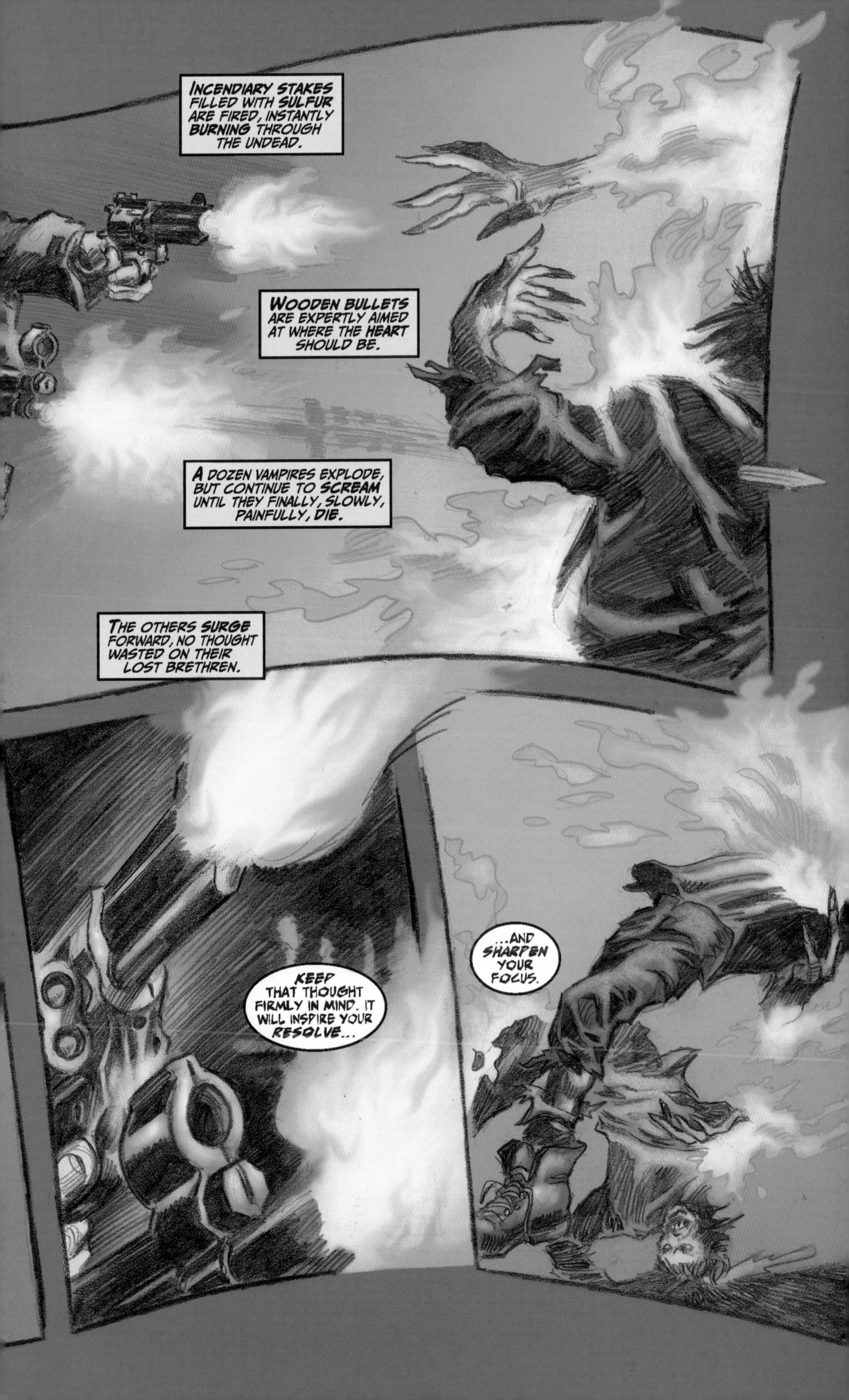
INCENDIARY STAKES FILLED WITH SULFUR ARE FIRED, INSTANTLY BURNING THROUGH THE UNDEAD.
WOODEN BULLETS ARE EXPERTLY AIMED AT WHERE THE HEART SHOULD BE.
A DOZEN VAMPIRES EXPLODE, BUT CONTINUE TO SCREAM UNTIL THEY FINALLY, SLOWLY, PAINFULLY, DIE.
THE OTHERS SURGE FORWARD, NO THOUGHT WASTED ON THEIR LOST BRETHREN.
KEEP THAT THOUGHT FIRMLY IN MIND. IT WILL INSPIRE YOUR RESOLVE...
...AND SHARPEN YOUR FOCUS.

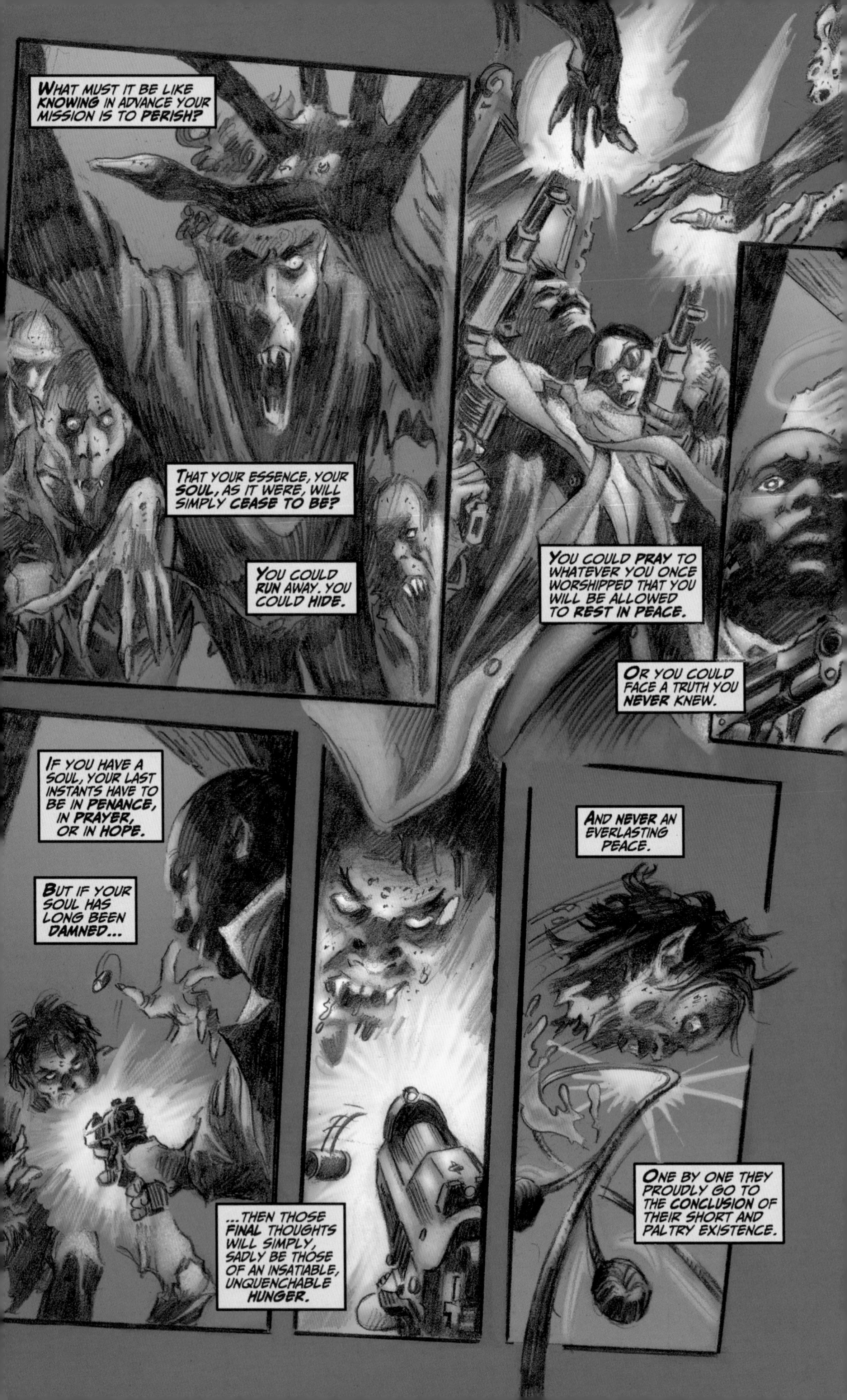
WHAT MUST IT BE LIKE KNOWING IN ADVANCE YOUR MISSION IS TO PERISH?
THAT YOUR ESSENCE, YOUR SOUL, AS IT WERE, WILL SIMPLY CEASE TO BE?
YOU COULD RUN AWAY. YOU COULD HIDE.
YOU COULD PRAY TO WHATEVER YOU ONCE WORSHIPPED THAT YOU WILL BE ALLOWED TO REST IN PEACE.
OR YOU COULD FACE A TRUTH YOU NEVER KNEW.
IF YOU HAVE A SOUL, YOUR LAST INSTANTS HAVE TO BE IN PENANCE, IN PRAYER, OR IN HOPE.
BUT IF YOUR SOUL HAS LONG BEEN DAMNED...
...THEN THOSE FINAL THOUGHTS WILL SIMPLY, SADLY BE THOSE OF AN INSATIABLE, UNQUENCHABLE HUNGER.
AND NEVER AN EVERLASTING PEACE.
ONE BY ONE THEY PROUDLY GO TO THE CONCLUSION OF THEIR SHORT AND PALTRY EXISTENCE.

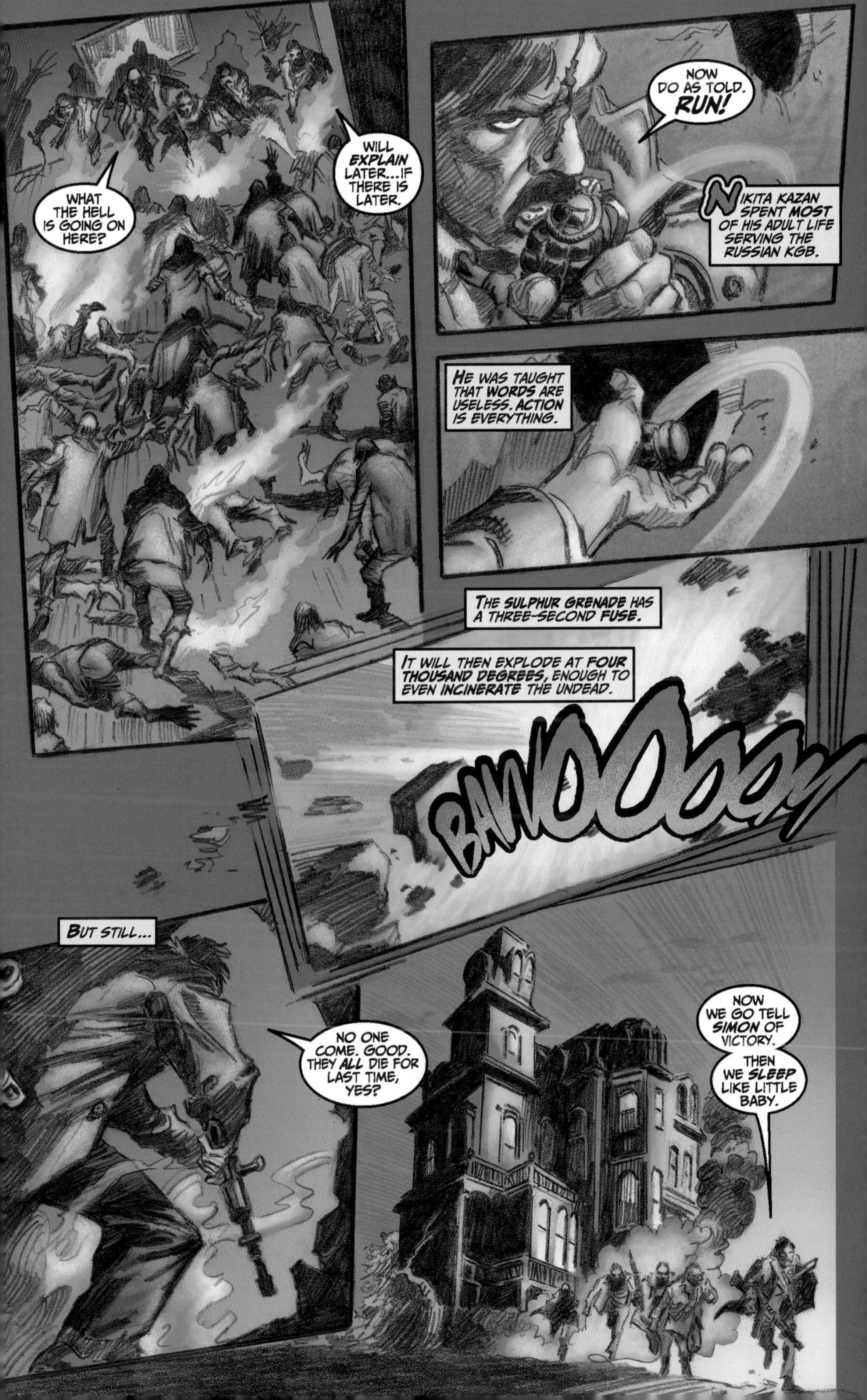
WHAT THE HELL IS GOING ON HERE?
WILL EXPLAIN LATER...IF THERE IS LATER.
NOW DO AS TOLD. RUN!
NIKITA KAZAN SPENT MOST OF HIS ADULT LIFE SERVING THE RUSSIAN KGB.
HE WAS TAUGHT THAT WORDS ARE USELESS. ACTION IS EVERYTHING.
THE SULPHUR GRENADE HAS A THREE-SECOND FUSE.
IT WILL THEN EXPLODE AT FOUR THOUSAND DEGREES, ENOUGH TO EVEN INCINERATE THE UNDEAD.
BAWOOOOM
BUT STILL...
NO ONE COME. GOOD. THEY ALL DIE FOR LAST TIME, YES?
NOW WE GO TELL SIMON OF VICTORY.
THEN WE SLEEP LIKE LITTLE BABY.

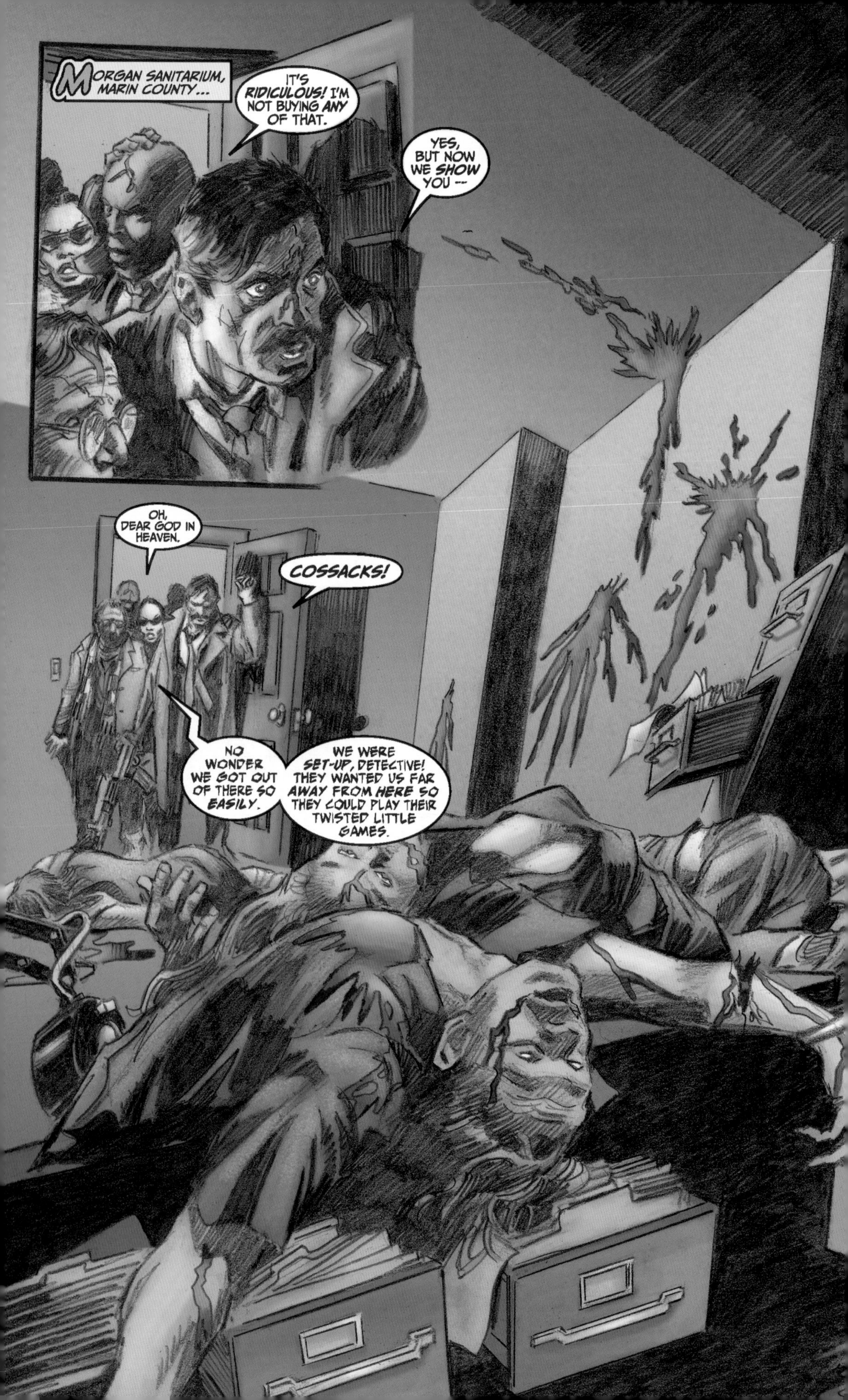
MORGAN SANITARIUM, MARIN COUNTY...
IT'S RIDICULOUS! I'M NOT BUYING ANY OF THAT.
YES, BUT NOW WE SHOW YOU ---
OH, DEAR GOD IN HEAVEN.
COSSACKS!
NO WONDER WE GOT OUT OF THERE SO EASILY.
WE WERE SET-UP, DETECTIVE! THEY WANTED US FAR AWAY FROM HERE SO THEY COULD PLAY THEIR TWISTED LITTLE GAMES.

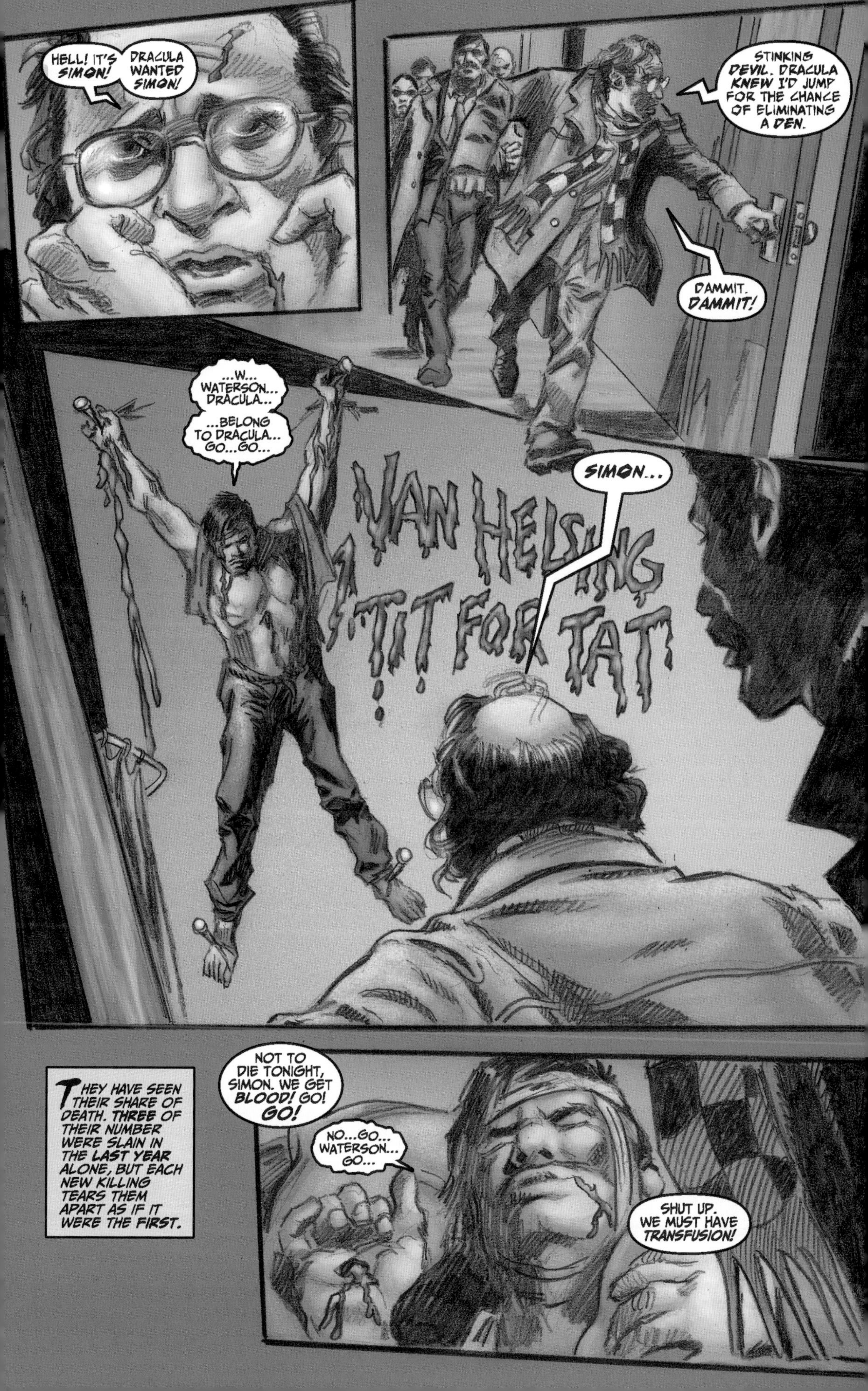
HELL! IT'S SIMON!
DRACULA WANTED SIMON!
STINKING DEVIL. DRACULA KNEW I'D JUMP FOR THE CHANCE OF ELIMINATING A DEN.
DAMMIT. DAMMIT!
...W... WATERSON... DRACULA...
...BELONG TO DRACULA... GO...GO...
VAN HELSING TIT FOR TAT
SIMON...
THEY HAVE SEEN THEIR SHARE OF DEATH. THREE OF THEIR NUMBER WERE SLAIN IN THE LAST YEAR ALONE, BUT EACH NEW KILLING TEARS THEM APART AS IF IT WERE THE FIRST.
NOT TO DIE TONIGHT, SIMON. WE GET BLOOD! GO! GO!
NO...GO... WATERSON... GO...
SHUT UP. WE MUST HAVE TRANSFUSION!

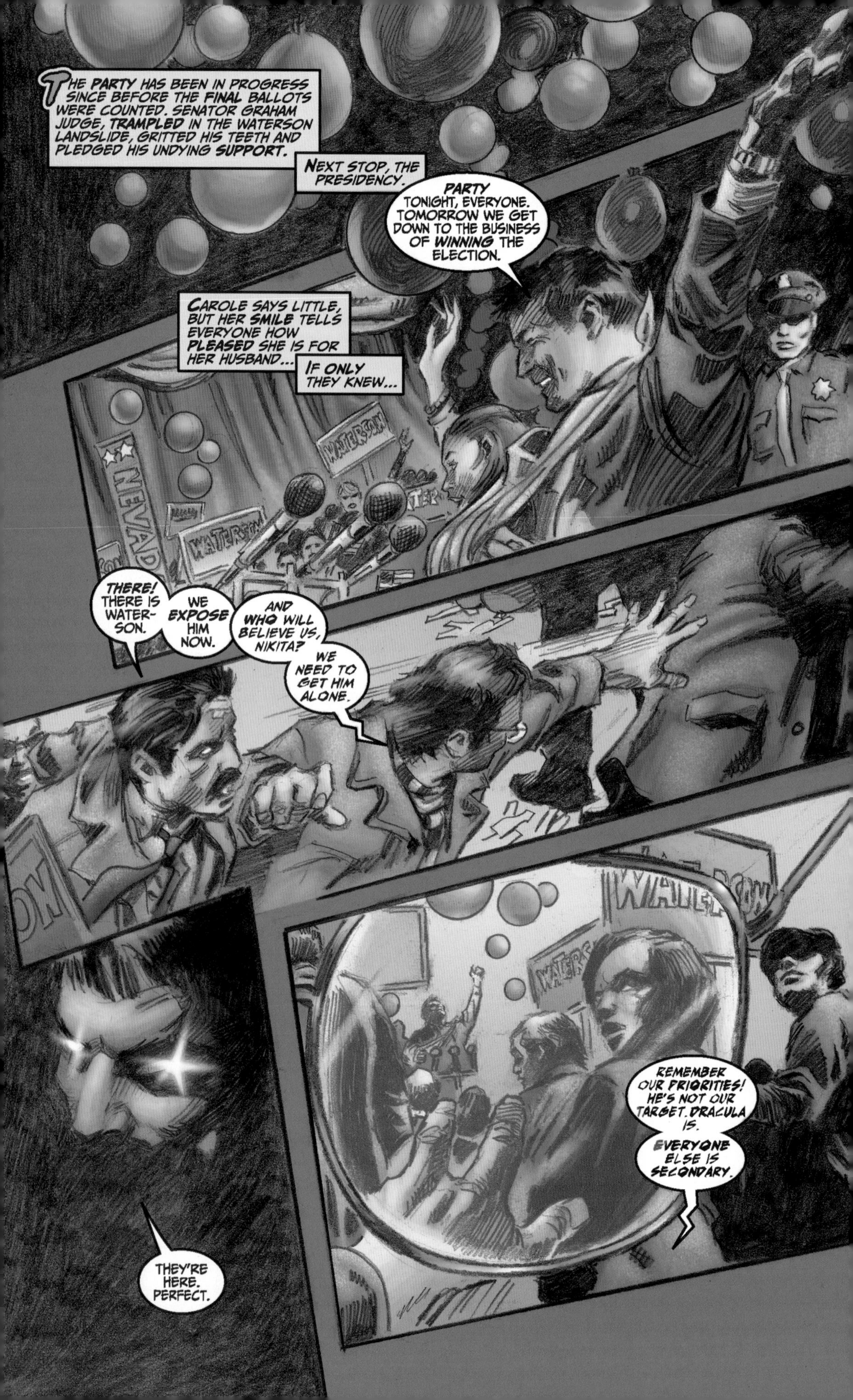
THE PARTY HAS BEEN IN PROGRESS SINCE BEFORE THE FINAL BALLOTS WERE COUNTED. SENATOR GRAHAM JUDGE, TRAMPLED IN THE WATERSON LANDSLIDE, GRITTED HIS TEETH AND PLEDGED HIS UNDYING SUPPORT.
NEXT STOP, THE PRESIDENCY.
PARTY TONIGHT, EVERYONE. TOMORROW WE GET DOWN TO THE BUSINESS OF WINNING THE ELECTION.
CAROLE SAYS LITTLE, BUT HER SMILE TELLS EVERYONE HOW PLEASED SHE IS FOR HER HUSBAND...
IF ONLY THEY KNEW...
WATERSON
NEVADA
WATERSON
THERE! THERE IS WATER-SON.
WE EXPOSE HIM NOW.
AND WHO WILL BELIEVE US, NIKITA?
WE NEED TO GET HIM ALONE.
THEY'RE HERE. PERFECT.
REMEMBER OUR PRIORITIES! HE'S NOT OUR TARGET. DRACULA IS.
EVERYONE ELSE IS SECONDARY.

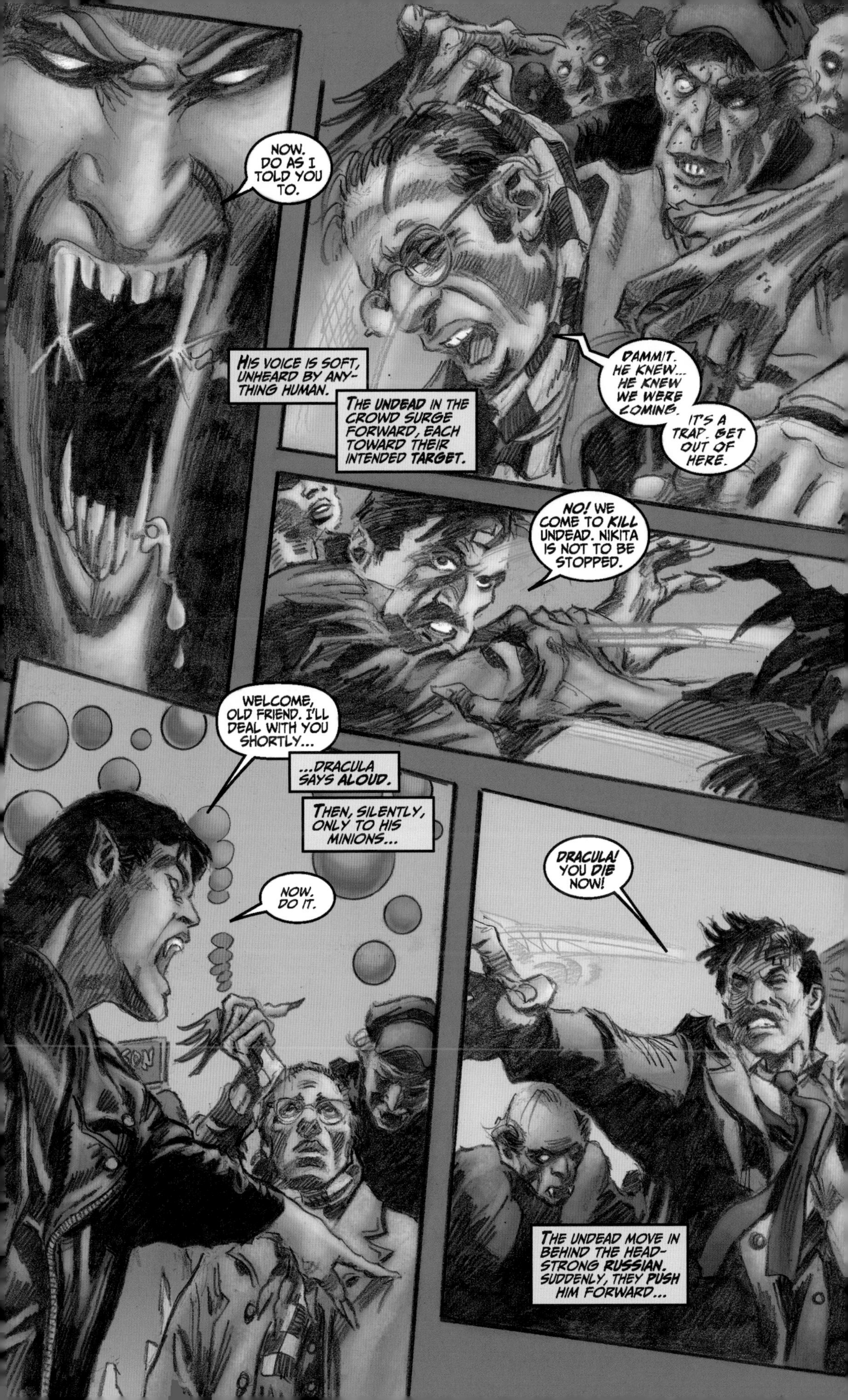
NOW. DO AS I TOLD YOU TO.
HIS VOICE IS SOFT, UNHEARD BY ANYTHING HUMAN.
THE UNDEAD IN THE CROWD SURGE FORWARD, EACH TOWARD THEIR INTENDED TARGET.
DAMMIT. HE KNEW... HE KNEW WE WERE COMING.
IT'S A TRAP. GET OUT OF HERE.
NO! WE COME TO KILL UNDEAD. NIKITA IS NOT TO BE STOPPED.
WELCOME, OLD FRIEND. I'LL DEAL WITH YOU SHORTLY...
...DRACULA SAYS ALOUD.
THEN, SILENTLY, ONLY TO HIS MINIONS...
NOW. DO IT.
DRACULA! YOU DIE NOW!
THE UNDEAD MOVE IN BEHIND THE HEADSTRONG RUSSIAN. SUDDENLY, THEY PUSH HIM FORWARD...

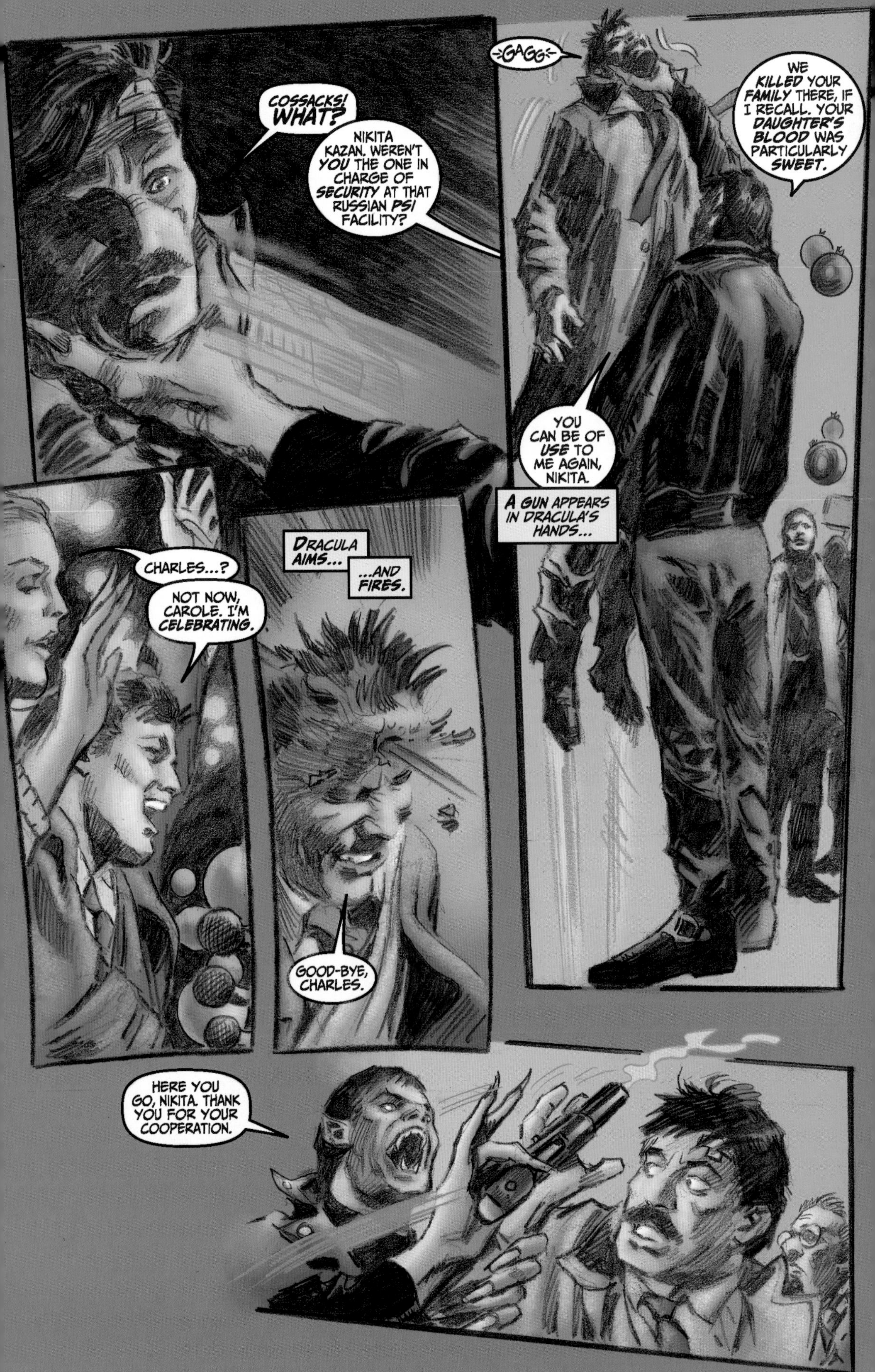
COSSACKS! WHAT?
NIKITA KAZAN. WEREN'T YOU THE ONE IN CHARGE OF SECURITY AT THAT RUSSIAN PSI FACILITY?
GAGG
WE KILLED YOUR FAMILY THERE, IF I RECALL. YOUR DAUGHTER'S BLOOD WAS PARTICULARLY SWEET.
YOU CAN BE OF USE TO ME AGAIN, NIKITA.
A GUN APPEARS IN DRACULA'S HANDS...
CHARLES...?
NOT NOW, CAROLE. I'M CELEBRATING.
DRACULA AIMS...
...AND FIRES.
GOOD-BYE, CHARLES.
HERE YOU GO, NIKITA. THANK YOU FOR YOUR COOPERATION.

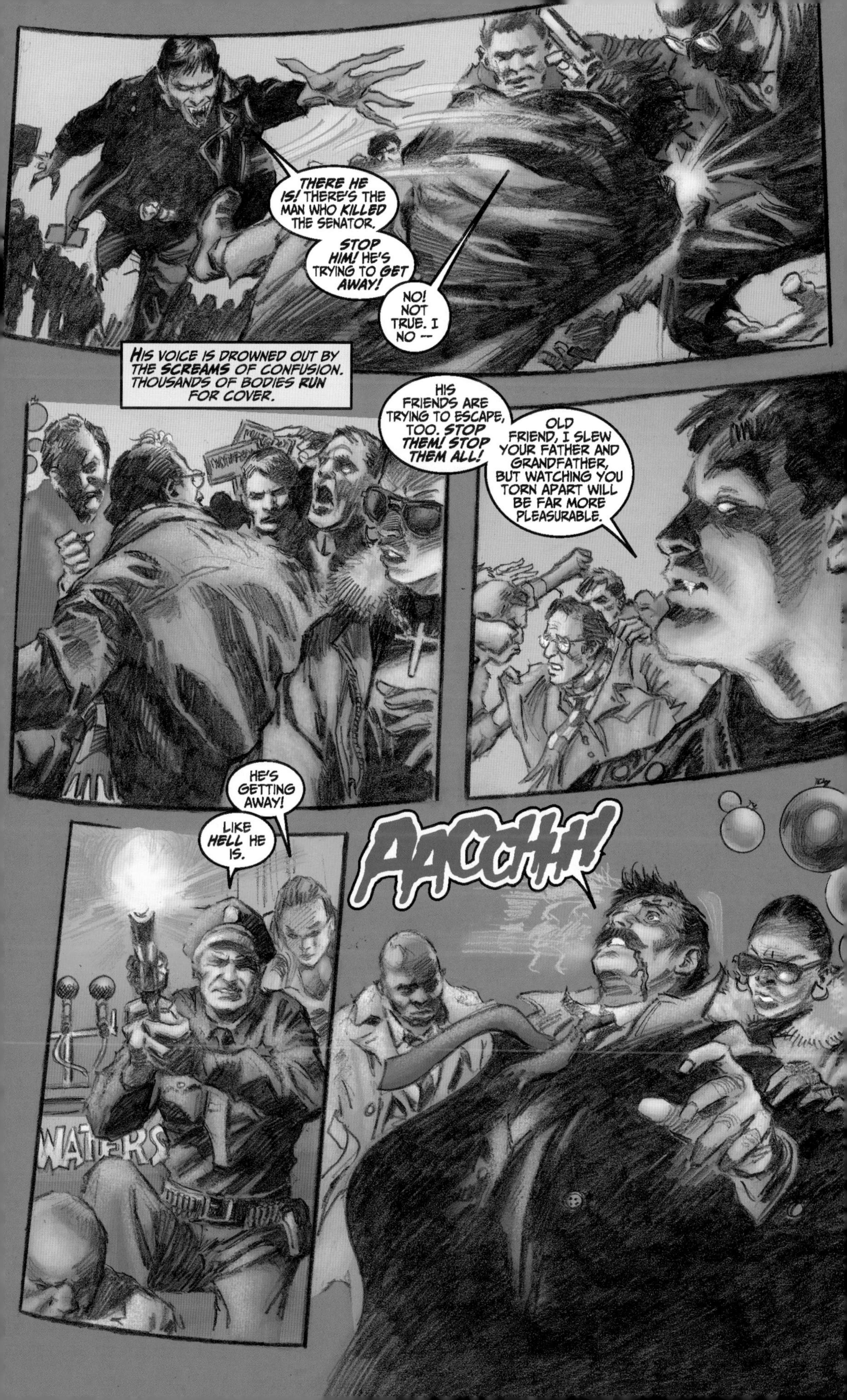
THERE HE IS! THERE'S THE MAN WHO KILLED THE SENATOR.
STOP HIM! HE'S TRYING TO GET AWAY!
NO! NOT TRUE. I NO --
HIS VOICE IS DROWNED OUT BY THE SCREAMS OF CONFUSION. THOUSANDS OF BODIES RUN FOR COVER.
HIS FRIENDS ARE TRYING TO ESCAPE, TOO. STOP THEM! STOP THEM ALL!
OLD FRIEND, I SLEW YOUR FATHER AND GRANDFATHER, BUT WATCHING YOU TORN APART WILL BE FAR MORE PLEASURABLE.
HE'S GETTING AWAY!
LIKE HELL HE IS.
AACCHH!
WATERS

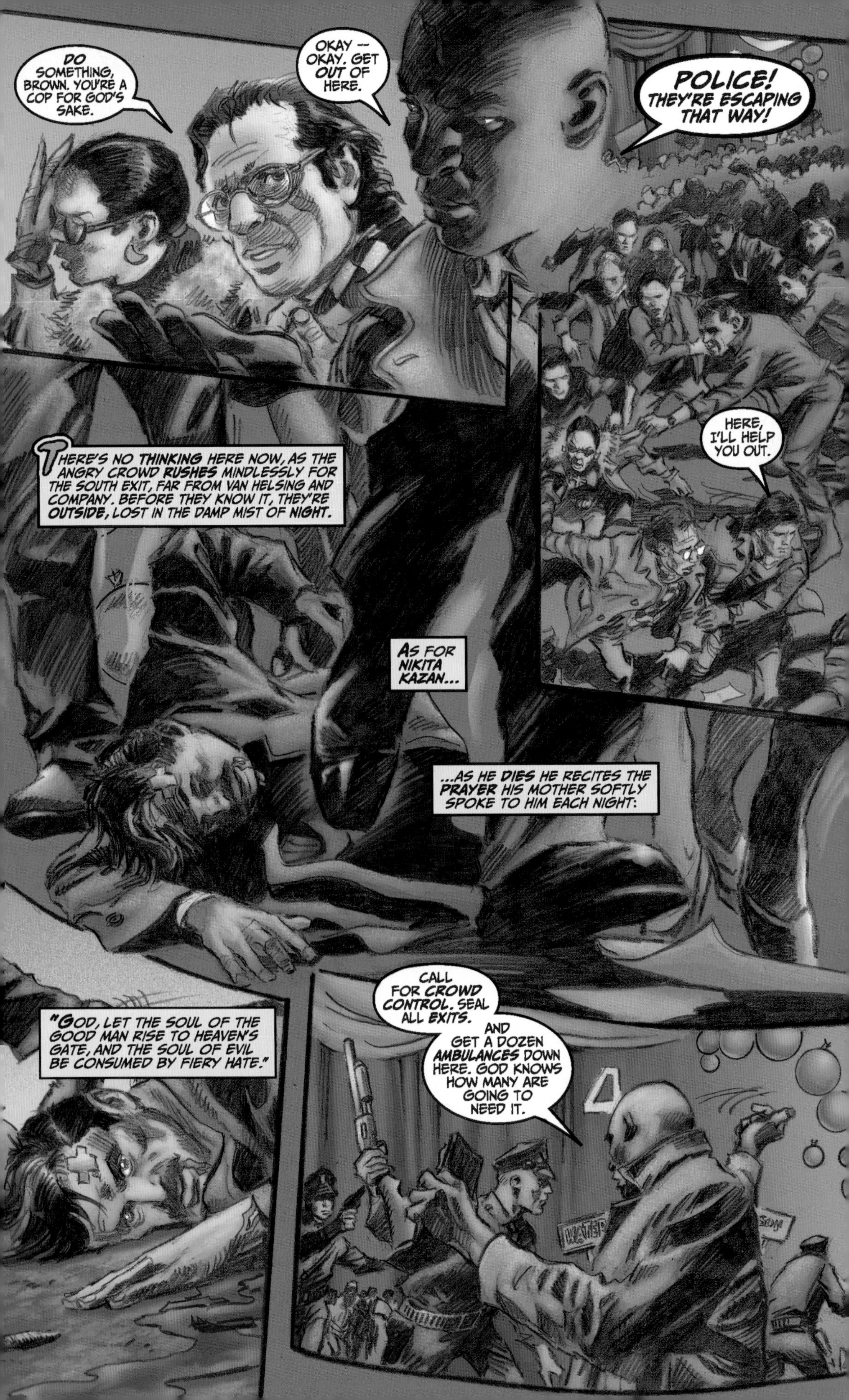
DO SOMETHING, BROWN. YOU'RE A COP FOR GOD'S SAKE.
OKAY -- OKAY. GET OUT OF HERE.
POLICE! THEY'RE ESCAPING THAT WAY!
THERE'S NO THINKING HERE NOW, AS THE ANGRY CROWD RUSHES MINDLESSLY FOR THE SOUTH EXIT, FAR FROM VAN HELSING AND COMPANY. BEFORE THEY KNOW IT, THEY'RE OUTSIDE, LOST IN THE DAMP MIST OF NIGHT.
HERE, I'LL HELP YOU OUT.
AS FOR NIKITA KAZAN...
...AS HE DIES HE RECITES THE PRAYER HIS MOTHER SOFTLY SPOKE TO HIM EACH NIGHT:
"GOD, LET THE SOUL OF THE GOOD MAN RISE TO HEAVEN'S GATE, AND THE SOUL OF EVIL BE CONSUMED BY FIERY HATE."
CALL FOR CROWD CONTROL. SEAL ALL EXITS.
AND GET A DOZEN AMBULANCES DOWN HERE. GOD KNOWS HOW MANY ARE GOING TO NEED IT.

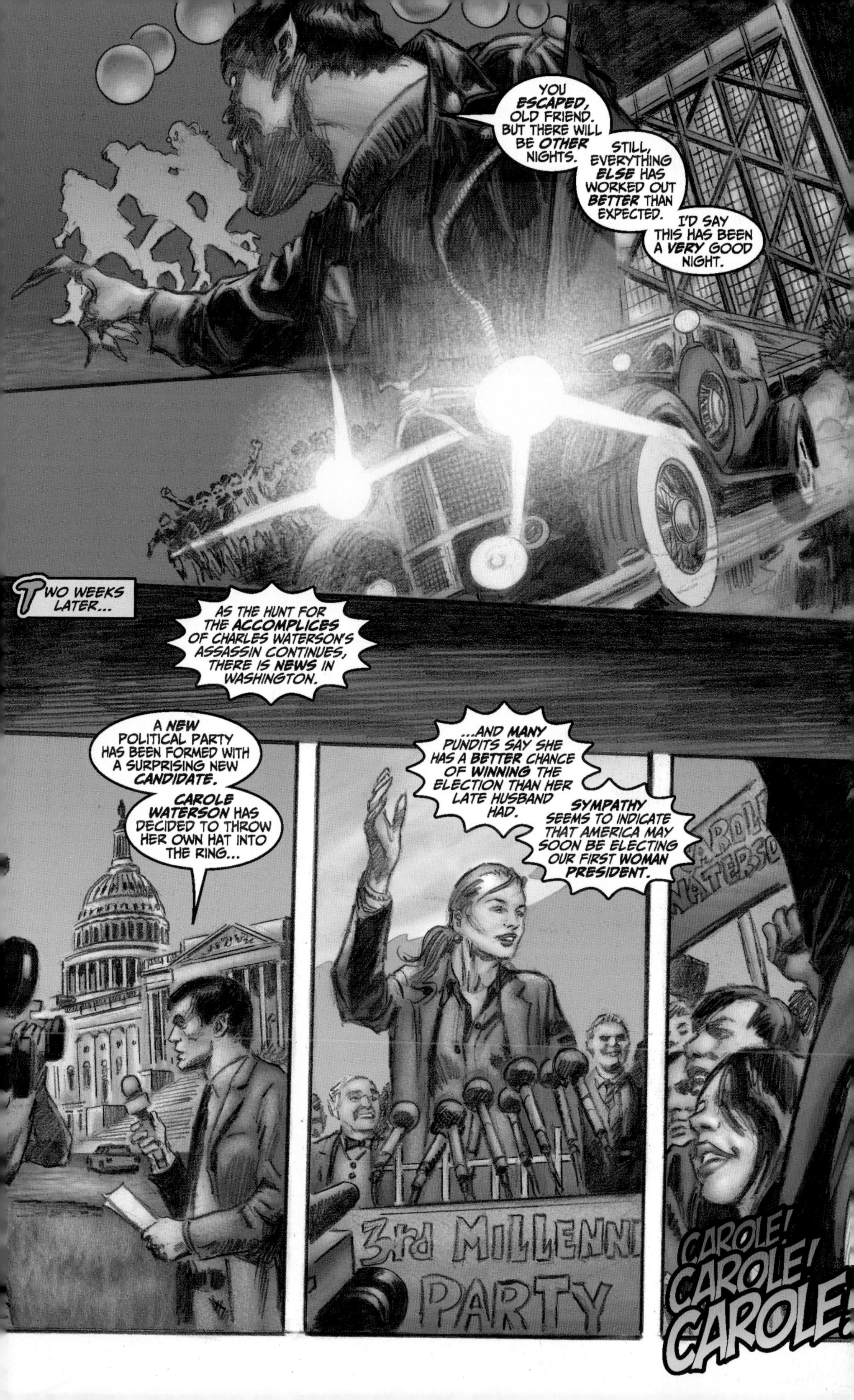
YOU ESCAPED, OLD FRIEND. BUT THERE WILL BE OTHER NIGHTS.
STILL, EVERYTHING ELSE HAS WORKED OUT BETTER THAN EXPECTED.
I'D SAY THIS HAS BEEN A VERY GOOD NIGHT.
TWO WEEKS LATER...
AS THE HUNT FOR THE ACCOMPLICES OF CHARLES WATERSON'S ASSASSIN CONTINUES, THERE IS NEWS IN WASHINGTON.
A NEW POLITICAL PARTY HAS BEEN FORMED WITH A SURPRISING NEW CANDIDATE.
CAROLE WATERSON HAS DECIDED TO THROW HER OWN HAT INTO THE RING...
...AND MANY PUNDITS SAY SHE HAS A BETTER CHANCE OF WINNING THE ELECTION THAN HER LATE HUSBAND HAD.
SYMPATHY SEEMS TO INDICATE THAT AMERICA MAY SOON BE ELECTING OUR FIRST WOMAN PRESIDENT.
3rd MILLENNI
PARTY
CAROLE! CAROLE! CAROLE!

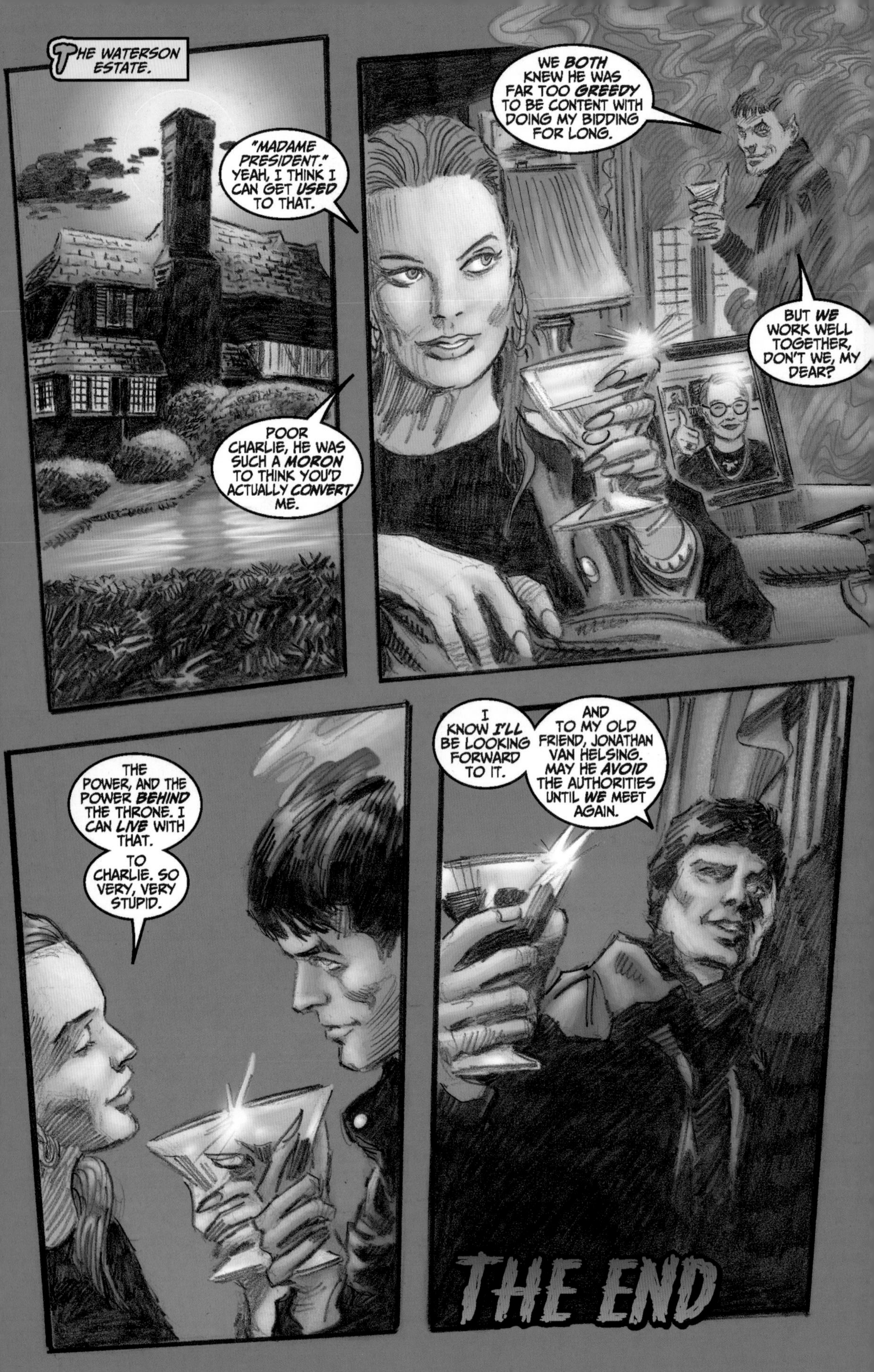
THE WATERSON ESTATE.
"MADAME PRESIDENT." YEAH, I THINK I CAN GET USED TO THAT.
POOR CHARLIE, HE WAS SUCH A MORON TO THINK YOU'D ACTUALLY CONVERT ME.
WE BOTH KNEW HE WAS FAR TOO GREEDY TO BE CONTENT WITH DOING MY BIDDING FOR LONG.
BUT WE WORK WELL TOGETHER, DON'T WE, MY DEAR?
THE POWER, AND THE POWER BEHIND THE THRONE. I CAN LIVE WITH THAT.
TO CHARLIE. SO VERY, VERY STUPID.
I KNOW I'LL BE LOOKING FORWARD TO IT.
AND TO MY OLD FRIEND, JONATHAN VAN HELSING. MAY HE AVOID THE AUTHORITIES UNTIL WE MEET AGAIN.
THE END